RADIANT

creating a deeper life

"RADIANT: Creating a Deeper Life" is a Canadian-based one-day women's conference designed to encourage Christian women towards becoming mature disciples of Jesus Christ—joyfully surrendered to His purpose for their lives, using their spiritual gifts to serve the local Church and engaged in outreach both within their community and abroad.

The conference package includes:

- worship music
- comedy
- biblical teaching about how to develop greater intimacy with God
- breakout sessions addressing topics including how to overcome abuse, how to find balance in a busy world, and how to grow an effective prayer life

RADIANT is a ministry of International Messengers Canada—a non-profit interdenominational organization that partners with more than 200 career missionaries in 20 countries.

Contact **info@RadiantWomen.ca** to learn more about RADIANT and how to host the conference in your community.

www.fb.com/RadiantCreatingADeeperLife

International Messengers (IM) is an evangelical interdenominational missions organization committed to making disciples of all nations. IM partners with local churches to renew, train and mobilize believers for active involvement in reaching the world for Christ.

Facts about International Messengers:

- Nearly 200 career missionaries serve in approximately 20 countries including Ukraine, Romania, Poland, Nepal, Egypt, Lithuania, and Peru.
- Specializes in relationship-based evangelism.
- Serves orphans, HIV/AIDS-infected youth, abused women and senior widows, Syrian refugees, Roma people (gypsies), university students, and many more.
- Trains missionaries in Uganda, Egypt, Ukraine, and North America.
- Offers a six-week summer internship for people ages 18-29.
- Offers three-month and two-year missions opportunities.
- Offers two-week summer mission projects—evangelistic English-learning summer camps. Includes training. Ideal for family involvement.

Contact **info@im-canada.ca** for more information about how you can get involved.

www.im-canada.ca

INTERNATIONAL
MESSENGERS
CANADA

Willms Seeds is honoured to sponsor "RADIANT: Creating a Deeper Life" to help Canadian women grow in their spiritual journey.

Willms Seeds is a family-owned and operated farm located near Grassy Lake, Alberta. Started by Henry and Verna Willms in 1956, its 320 original acres produced pedigreed wheat.

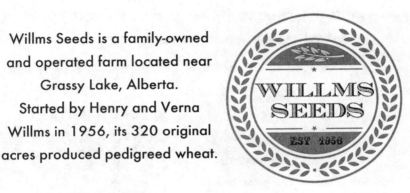

Henry's son Tim began farming with his dad in 1984 and purchased his own land two years later. Eventually Tim assumed the farm's management. Tim and his wife Michelle have three children—Matthew, Austin, and Mya.

The operation has grown to 12,500 acres and now produces many different crops: soft wheat, barley, durum, flax and pulses (peas, lentils, chickpeas, fababeans, soybeans). Their quality pedigreed seeds are sold to other farmers across Canada.

Contact Tim at **tim@willmsseeds.com** or call 403-634-4155.

https://twitter.com/willmsseeds

We're delighted to partner with
"RADIANT: Creating a Deeper Life"
to give this gift to women across Canada.
What a terrific opportunity to bring you hope and
encouragement from Canadian writers whose work
is distinguished by honesty and vulnerability!
And who might well be your neighbours.

Hot Apple Cider books are gifts that keep giving!

If you enjoy reading
A Taste of Hot Apple Cider,
we'd like to offer you
a second, even bigger book,
FREE as an ebook!
You'll also get reader updates
and special offers.

Hot Apple Cider: Words to Warm the Soul and Stir the Heart has
44 stories of hope and encouragement by 30 writers

Download your second gift book at:

http://hotapplaciderbooks.com/subscribe/

Books that integrate real life with real faith

Hot Apple Cider

"A collection of short stories, poetry, and wisdom seeking to heal and mend the soul of the reader after difficult and stressful situations.... Highly recommended."
Midwest Book Review

"Along with the heartwarming, real-life stories...the editors of this collection have tossed in some surprises. There is poetry, short fiction, and some tart essays on drug addiction, poverty, and the plight of Third World women."
Mennonite Brethren Herald

"Much in the tradition of *Chicken Soup for the Soul*, these delightful readings are like a cozy cup of hot cider. Settle in for a moment of warmth and reflection.... Enjoy!"
Brian C. Stiller, Global Ambassador for the World Evangelical Alliance

"One of the gripping and disturbing things [in this book] is the collective pain. But even more gripping is the collective hope and triumph that rises through the pain.... I don't think a resource for grieving people was one of the primary purposes of this book, but I think it is one of the best I have read."
Brian Austin, author of *Muninn's Keep*

"If you're looking for inspiration, something to breathe in for reassurance that you're not alone, something to remind you to hear God's voice in acts of compassion, spend an afternoon with *Hot Apple Cider*. It could just change your life."
Jane Kirkpatrick, award-winning author of *All Together in One Place*

"Whether you sip *Hot Apple Cider* slowly, one story at a time, or drink deeply and read it all in one sitting, these stories of fun, faith and fellowship by gifted Canadian writers will warm your heart."
Dave Toycen, President and CEO, World Vision Canada

Winner, five The Word Awards

**Winner, Church Library Association of Ontario
One Book/One Conference**

A Second Cup of Hot Apple Cider

"Some books surprise you with their ability to take your breath away... The short selections make this a perfect book for even indifferent readers.... Be sure to buy more than one, for you will probably have the urge to share this gem of a collection with others."
Faith Today

"Short stories, poetry, and works of memoir picked for their inspirational nature, dedicated to finding a shining light in our lives that so often turn dark...touching and poignant."
Midwest Book Review

"From a host of talented writers who serve rich words, wrap your hands around a volume that will not only warm you right through, but strengthen you for the road ahead. A perfectly inspiring read."
Ann Voskamp, author of *New York Times* bestselling book *One Thousand Gifts*

"Hope-filled nuggets of wisdom...deep and soulful and pleasing."
Manitoba Christian Online

"What a great book! [It] will give you a refreshing lift and a change of perspective, perhaps when you need it most."
Ellen Vaughn, *New York Times* bestselling author

"This collection of wonderful writing...is honest, personal, and compelling.... Like me, you'll be comforted, inspired, and encouraged. I felt as if God were reading over my shoulder."
Michael Messenger, Executive VP, World Vision Canada

"This comforting and encouraging book should be in every home, library, church, and school."
Pauline Christian, President, Black Business and Professional Association

Winner, thirteen The Word Awards

Winner, Christian Small Publisher Gift Book of the Year

Winner, third place, The Book Club Network, Inc. Book of the Year

A Taste of
Hot Apple
Cider

WORDS *to* ENCOURAGE *and* INSPIRE

Edited by

N. J. LINDQUIST

That's Life! Communications

Markham, Ontario

A Taste of Hot Apple Cider

That's Life! Communications
Box 77001, Markham, ON L3P 0C8, Canada
905-471-1447
http://thatslifecommunications.com
comments@thatslifecommunications.com

ISBN: 978-1-927692-12-7

Cover design and interior layout by N. J. Lindquist.
Photo on page 101 © Kimberley Payne
Photos from Dreamstime.com:
© Denira777 | Dreamstime.com - Apple Photo
© Zhushev | Dreamstime.com - Apple Juice Still Life Photo
© Annatv81 | Dreamstime.com - Apple Tree Branch In Bloom Photo
© Irinaroibu | Dreamstime.com - Green And Yellow Apples On The White In The Form Of A Triangle Billiard Photo
© Evgenyi44 | Dreamstime.com - Apples Small Size On A White Background Photo
© Nobil2 | Dreamstime.com - Red And Yellow Apples In The Basket Photo
© Merkushev | Dreamstime.com - Yellow Apples In A Wicker Basket Photo
© Zannahol | Dreamstime.com - Crow Sitting On Apple Tree Photo
Any other photos used are from iStockphoto.

Library and Archives Canada Cataloguing in Publication
A taste of hot apple cider : words to encourage and inspire / edited by N.J. Lindquist.
Issued in print and electronic formats.
ISBN 978-1-927692-12-7 (pbk.).--ISBN 978-1-927692-13-4 (html)
    1. Inspiration--Religious aspects--Christianity. 2. Christian life--Anecdotes.
3. Spiritual life--Anecdotes. 4. Canadian literature
(English)--Christian authors. I. Lindquist, N. J. (Nancy J.), 1948-, editor
BV4515.3.T38 2014   242   C2014-906970-7
                                      C2014-906971-5

This book is dedicated to everyone who has a story to tell.
Yes, that means you.

Table of Contents

Foreword

Grace Fox

Life's challenges often blow in when least expected.

Some folks attempt to escape the storm, only to discover its gale force winds can't be outrun.

Others deny its existence, hoping to restore the day-to-day's usual and comfortable course by ignoring what's happening around them.

Then there are the ones who charge ahead, going against the winds, only to end up exhausted and embittered.

But a few people rise on the currents and embrace the storm as an opportunity to see life from a heavenly perspective.

These men and women inspire me. Their stories, told with down-to-earth warmth and vulnerability, urge me to keep the faith. They stir me to see the good in a scenario that, at first glimpse, appears only bad. They encourage me to consider every difficulty a chance to develop perseverance and godly maturity. And they remind me that our trying experiences are designed for more than our personal growth. They're meant to be told to benefit others—to shine a ray of hope into the darkness, to toss a lifeline to a sinking soul.

The contributors to *A Taste of Hot Apple Cider* fall into this category of inspirational men and women. Through poems, fiction, and nonfiction alike, they remind readers that the struggles we face are common to man. Their honest descriptions of wrestling with cancer, caring for and losing aging parents, dealing with a spouse's dementia, moving beyond one's fear to tell neighbours about Jesus, and more, show us that hope is very much alive. That hope is able to help us not only survive, but thrive, in the midst of whatever challenges we encounter.

I trust you'll find these stories as uplifting as I did. Consider going deeper by inviting a friend or small group to participate in the study questions included.

If you haven't already read *Hot Apple Cider* and *A Second Cup of Hot Apple Cider*, then now's the time to order them—you'll enjoy them, too.

Read on, my friend. And know you are loved.

Grace Fox

Grace Fox's passion is to help her audiences connect the dots between faith and real life. She's a popular international speaker at women's events in North America, Asia, and Eastern Europe. She's the award-winning author of eight books including *Morning Moments With God: Devotions for the Busy Woman*.

Together with her husband, Grace co-directs International Messengers Canada, a ministry with 180 career missionaries in 15 countries, and leads several short-term missions trips each year.

Visit her website (www.gracefox.com) for more information about her books and speaking topics.

Introduction

The first two books we published in the Hot Apple Cider series—*Hot Apple Cider* and *A Second Cup of Hot Apple Cider*—have both become Canadian bestsellers. In addition, 30,000 copies of each book have been given out through World Vision Canada. However, we know that there are still many more readers who would love these books but haven't yet discovered them.

So, we decided to publish a shorter book which, while able to stand on its own, could serve as an introduction to the whole series, including the forthcoming *Hot Apple Cider with Cinnamon*, coming in 2015.

As was the case with our first books, we sought out strong stories that were well-told. Our goal is not only to entertain, but also to encourage and inspire readers.

Inside, you'll find 16 terrific pieces (personal stories, poetry and fiction) by 15 Canadian writers. All of the contributors in this shorter book were also in one or both of the previous editions.

Each piece in this book is honest and heartfelt, as are the pieces in our other books. You'll also find photographs and biographies of each of the writers, and the questions at the back of the book will either help you get more out of the stories on your own or guide your book club or small group discussions.

Taking time to sit back and savour a cup of hot apple cider is something that makes most of us slow down and relax. Not only is the drink actually nutritious, but the break, too, is restorative. That's how we see the Hot Apple Cider series: as offering both nutrition and restoration for our mental and spiritual health.

So take a break, read a short piece or two, and restore your soul at the same time.

We trust you'll not only enjoy this book but also want to share it with others.

Les Lindquist, partner, That's Life! Communications

Subway Surprise

Nonfiction

A. A. Adourian

It's a chilly Monday morning in March as I head up, then down, a combination of stairs and escalators toward the westbound train platform at Victoria Park subway station in Toronto. The only thing that might make this commute even colder would be if I really were on a roller coaster—going up and down at break-neck speed. *Why is Canada always so cold?*

Finally on the platform—at the wrong end; no surprise since my thoughts are definitely taking some wrong turns this morning— I walk to the other end as the whistling sound of arctic winds often overpowers the sustained hum of rolling wheels on smooth concrete. Suitcases! My left foot narrowly escapes an unwieldy grey one. I always seem to walk behind people with suitcases. *Where are all these people going?*

Now, waiting for the train, the word "community" jumps out from subway wall art in English, but also in letters from languages that are foreign to me. *Lord, where is my community? Where do I fit? You know I have to have certain conversations that I don't want to have, and I have to make difficult decisions I don't want to make. And then there's my job situation. It isn't desperate, but it might be if something doesn't change...*

Alone on the platform, I sense that my "community" is my backpack, my purse, and the heavy tango of the words "change" and "future" dancing through my thoughts.

The longer I wait, the more hopeless I feel. I remind myself how counting on what people promise, and expecting solutions from them—when only God has the answers—only leads to disappointment. I know God hasn't forgotten me, but with every well-meaning option that doesn't pan out, and every broken promise,

I feel more forgotten. *Lord, why don't You do something? Just do something?*

"Wait, one mee-nut," says a voice I think is talking to me. I quickly look to my right and see a mother grasping for her daughter's wiggling hand.

Glancing further down the platform, I see the usual rainbow of human skin colours, typically adorned in black, navy, or grey, occasionally broken up by a purple Mohawk, a prematurely balding head, a jungle-patterned skirt, or a multi-coloured sari (thankfully not all on one person). *Where's the guy with his cat on a leash?* He wears that Siamese like a furry turtleneck until it starts to wag its tail.

Finally seated on the crowded train, trying to place the faintly familiar scent—paint, garbage, gas…and the sound—Eminem or the latest hit from Bollywood—I see a man and boy, probably father and son, playing Crazy Eights. I don't think I've seen card games played live on the subway before—it is usually some form of Solitaire via a handheld gadget.

I sit back and shut my eyes for a moment. I guess this is "community" these days: too much of everything all around vying for my attention, taking my focus, draining me. Indeed, a mix of Crazy Eights and Solitaire, when I think about it.

Then I open my eyes to see a jeans-clad middle-aged woman, standing in front of me but to the left. Morning commuters usually stand still and stay silent. But the sound of the train humming along the tracks seems to accompany this woman as she sways back and forth in her sneakers, holding on to the pole in front of her with both hands. Her offbeat swaying and the smile on her face make her look out of place. I look away in case she's smiling at me because she wants my seat. *It is Monday and I am tired, Lord,* I reason with God.

The subway and its platform (the place where you "stand well back of the yellow line as the train approaches") is the kind of place where kindness is rare; a sardine-like travel experience is par for the course and giving up your seat is the epitome of sacrifice.

"Sorry" doesn't really count on the subway—most people slam against each other without so much as an acknowledgement.

  A Taste of Hot Apple Cider

The ones who do say "sorry" hardly care to hear the "that's okay" that is sometimes said in response. Big mistakes—such as falling on another person because the train brakes suddenly—those merit a polite, if embarrassed, exchange. It is, after all, the driver's fault.

Tilting my head, I see the woman out of the corner of my eye. She's still swaying. How can she move like that on a Monday morning? I feel weaker than usual and hungry to the core of my soul.

I quickly open the small *Our Daily Bread* booklet that I read in the mornings, and go to the Bible passage for the day. It's a familiar one to me. The parable of the talents (Matthew 25:14-21). Talents. I want to use my talents for God, but there is just so much to consider. *How am I going to talk to...? What about my job, Lord? What do I say if she says...? And when will I know if...?* I keep praying, silently begging God to show me His plan for my life, where I'm going and what I'm supposed to be doing.

I hear a new sound and realize this same woman is singing in a very low voice, repeating what sounds like "Jesus."

Now, you've really lost it, I think. *You want to hear from God so desperately that you're imagining things.*

Discreetly, I watch her and notice that she seems to be accompanied by another woman—possibly her more fashionable sister—and a younger man. They all stand together, though the other two are standing still. Sometimes they talk, exchanging words in a language I don't know. I sense there is something about her, but I have no idea what it is. I lower my head so people don't see me crying and hear me whispering, "Please speak, Lord, speak, speak, speak..."

"The next station is Bay. Bay Station. Arriving at," with a slight two-second pause, "Bay Station." *No, that's not You speaking, Lord.*

As I prepare to exit, I discover that the woman is now in front of me, angled to my right. I barely have time to ask myself why she would move toward me and farther away from the train doors before she leans down to tap me on my right shoulder.

I look up at her pock-marked, swarthy, red-lipped face and hear her say, gently, "I just want to let you know Jesus loves you."

In a split second, I realize that some part of me felt her praying and worshipping as she swayed. I somehow manage a stunned, "I love Him, too!"

"Amen!" She lowers her voice. "I haven't ridden the subway in twenty years. Maybe I did today just to tell you these words."

Overwhelmed, I say thank you through my tears.

As I exit the train, I am, for the first time in a long while, thankful for the throng of people ahead of me that gives me an excuse to linger in His presence. Inside, I'm twirling and leaping like a ballerina. *Lord, You spoke! You spoke! You spoke! Help me always remember that we're in this life together, that my talents belong to You, and that even when I have no idea what's going to happen next, I trust You.*

    A Taste of Hot Apple Cider

Love Has No Limits

Nonfiction

Donna Fawcett

"So…I was just waiting for Bill to take me to the airport to fly back home when the phone rang. I guess a friend from the old school asked if I had a girlfriend. You know Bill… didn't even cover the phone…just bellowed out, 'Ed! You got a girlfriend?' I told him, 'No'. This friend of ours said she'd given my phone number to one of her girlfriends—that this girlfriend would likely call me. Her name is Bell. I doubt she'll call…"

As I pulled the van out of the Hamilton airport parking lot, I heard the mixture of hope and doubt as his voice trailed off. For a moment I felt as if I'd stepped back in time to the locker-riddled halls of my high school years, but the speaker here, stumbling over tentative words, was no pimple-faced teen. This was my eighty-two-year-old father.

Fifty-four years of marriage had abruptly ended in the quagmire of cancer and now, four years later, he still walked, unprepared, through life as a solo act.

Dad's visits to Halifax to see his identical twin brother, Bill, and Bill's wife, May, had been the only thing keeping him interested in life. Together, they attended a weekly jamboree and sing-along during each three-week stay.

A part of me struggled with the idea of a possible replacement for our mother. Most of me recognized the quiet despair behind Dad's words. He wore his loneliness like a shroud.

Dad's chatter filled the hour-long drive to our home north of London. I watched him drag his suitcase through the sunroom toward the granny flat we had added to our house for my parents several years earlier, and I wondered if it would become home to a new step-mom. Could I handle that?

As he unlocked his door, the excitement dimmed a bit and he looked at me through lost eyes. "She probably won't call, but it's nice to think she was interested."

I put as much enthusiasm into my voice as I could muster. "I think it's great, Dad. I'm sure she'll call you."

My words brought back the smile and excitement to a face void of those expressions for far too long. What would my siblings think? Would they be upset? Not all of my four brothers and sister were there when Mom had said not to let Dad be alone for long. I didn't know how any of us would react if the time came to accept a new family member.

"If she calls, let everyone else know, okay? They'll be happy for you, too." I hoped my words carried the truth.

Later, I shared my concerns with my husband, Jeff. In his patient wisdom, he reminded me that the best thing I could do was pray and trust in Dad's judgement. Easier said than done.

I busied myself with the mundane tasks of housework while my mind churned through "what-if's." My heart ached for the man who had once been vibrant and full of zest for life. Since Mom's death he'd shuffled through the motions of life like an automaton. Having a girlfriend might be a very good thing. He'd begun to look thin—thinner than his slim frame could afford. Maybe she'd fatten him up a bit. I smiled. It might be just what he needed.

The next afternoon, a knock on our sunroom door told me Dad had come for his regular three o'clock coffee break. The door wasn't yet all the way open when he burst out with his news. "She called! Bell called! Her name's really Isabel. She's my age and she's been watching me at the hootenannies and—wait 'til I tell you this!" He shut the door, strode to his spot at the kitchen table, and continued tossing out jumbled sentences.

I poured coffee while he bubbled on. "Bell didn't even know her friend had called Bill. She'd mentioned she saw me and thought I was handsome. She said she was pretty embarrassed to find out about the phone call to Bill and me. I told her it was okay and I was glad she called. We talked for a long time. It's amazing how much we know about each other just through common friends. She was married to a soldier too—just like your mother and me."

  A Taste of Hot Apple Cider

My heart beat a bit faster. I hadn't seen this much energy pour from Dad since before Mom's last days. He dithered and shifted, crossing and uncrossing restless legs—drumming nervous fingers to an invisible beat. It was as though his batteries were overcharged. My father, in all his frenetic energy, had awakened from the walking coma he'd lived in for four years. I listened as his animated conversation spilled out every detail.

"I told her she'd have to send me a picture since I can't remember what she looked like. She said we met once, but I met a lot of people at those music nights. I don't recall half of them. She's going to call again tonight since she's got a good long distance phone plan." He grinned—really grinned—and his eyes danced. "I asked her if she'd like a picture of me and she said, 'No Ed. I see your look-alike every Saturday night when I watch Bill sing and play the guitar.' I forgot about Bill being there. So she's going to mail me a picture."

I swallowed hard and sat listening to Dad rattle on for the next half hour before he stood to go. "I shouldn't stay long. You'll need to get supper on for Jeff and I want to get the barn cats fed early so I don't miss her call."

I watched, shell-shocked, as he breezed back out into the sunroom, marched to his apartment door, and slipped on the battered running shoes he wore in the tractor shed where the cats lived. A brief wave of the hand and he was out the door and cutting across the lawn.

I glanced at the clock. The hands had just shifted to four p.m. Dad had said that Bell wasn't supposed to call until nine that night. The cats usually weren't fed until seven p.m. They wouldn't know what hit them.

For the next month and a half, we settled into a routine. Dad would feed the cats early, eat a quick five o'clock supper at his favourite diner, stop by for an evening coffee, update Jeff and me on Bell's life, and wait in jittery excitement for nine to come. Being old-fashioned, he didn't feel right about Bell calling him, so he upgraded his phone plan and insisted on calling her.

I learned much about my father during those coffee breaks. He and Bell had quickly settled into a camaraderie that allowed them to share any subject that came to mind. They talked about their deceased spouses. They talked about gardening. They talked about their faith in God and how He had carried them through the loss of their loved ones. No subject was left untouched. And most of their conversations were shared with us.

It didn't surprise me at all when, one afternoon in late October, Dad announced that he was flying back out east. "We've become quite attached to each other and figured we should probably meet before we let ourselves get too serious."

I fought a smile. I couldn't decide whether this was a twist to the modern internet dating or a step back into the era of matchmaking. "I think that's a great idea. When do you want to go?"

"I have my flight booked for next Thursday."

I gripped my coffee cup tighter, fearing I might drop it.

As though reading my mind, he grinned. "They don't call me 'Fast Eddie' for nothing."

I laughed and shook my head. "Have you told the others?"

"Everyone knows about Bell and they all gave me their approval."

The fact that all six of us kids had agreed that Dad needed this was all the confirmation he needed to move forward—something he might not have done if any of us objected. While none of us had yet met Bell, everything Dad had told us about her, combined with his renewed zest for life, assured us that she'd be good for him.

A week later, I drove Dad to the airport, wondering what would come of his fourteen days away. He figured it would only take that long to be sure she was the one for him.

He called when he landed to let us know he'd made it. I could hear a new level of excitement in his voice and I threw a prayer heavenward that this wouldn't be a disappointment for him. I struggled to know how to pray for a relationship which could end in a step-mother trying to fill the void left by my mother. What if Bell wasn't what she seemed to be?

The time dragged by, broken only by a couple of brief phone calls from Halifax. I thought often of my father and his romantic adventure. What if it came to nothing? How would I help an eighty-two-year-old recover from rejection?

I could barely wait to pick him up from the airport. I'd planned to have lunch with him on the way home so I could find out everything, but before we'd even arrived at the restaurant, I'd already heard enough to know that this was no fly-by-night relationship.

"I was waiting for Bill to pick me up at the airport," he told me, "when this lovely, white-haired lady slipped in beside me and said, 'Hello.' Bell came to the airport to meet me! I thought it was just the nicest thing she could've done. Bill thought I should go back to his place in her car but she insisted that we boys drive together and she'd meet us there. When we got there, she and May really hit it off."

Once we were seated at our regular table in the diner we visited on occasion, Dad got right down to business. "What would you think about us getting married?"

My coffee cup rattled as I set it down. The shock faded quickly, though. What could I say? I knew what Mom would say. *Finally, he's not alone anymore!* My tongue came unglued. "I think that would be great, Dad."

"It's not like we're teenagers and all mushy with emotion. We've talked about everything. I feel like I've known her for years. She's a wonderful lady. I'm lucky."

I bit into my burger and nodded my agreement.

"What would you think about next week?"

When my coughing fit ended and I'd swallowed enough water to dilute any vestiges of masticated beef patty, I wiped my eyes and chose my words carefully. "Why so soon?" It was probably the dumbest question out of my mouth that day.

"I'm eighty-two. She's eighty-two. We're not getting any younger. If we're going to have any time together at all, we can't procrastinate."

Bell's family had had plenty of time to get to know Dad during his visit east. So they'd decided that when Bell flew to Ontario, she could meet us, get married, and settle into the apartment. Then they'd have a second wedding ceremony in Halifax in the spring.

I nodded in an imitation of a dashboard bobble-head doll and then sputtered out the only thing I could think of. "You'd better call the family. And you might want to put it off an extra week so we can all get to know Bell first."

Dad thought about that and nodded his agreement. "Okay, can we stop and talk to Dave and make some arrangements?" Dave, Dad's minister, would likely wear the same stunned expression that must have been draped across my features at that moment. I swallowed hard, realizing I was about to have the craziest two weeks I'd ever had. And that it would end with the addition of a second mother plus five new siblings and their spouses, children, and grandchildren to our family.

Bell arrived a week later, which gave me a chance to prepare our guest room and arrange for the upcoming wedding.

Jeff and I knew within five minutes of visiting with Bell that God had chosen this wonderful woman to fill the gap in Dad's world. Her enthusiasm for life gripped us. Her humour delighted us. Her laughter was contagious. I understood immediately what Dad had meant when he'd said he felt he'd known her forever.

The autumn days sped by and the weather began its shift into lower temperatures. We had a family gathering and Bell won the hearts of us all.

Bell's daughter, Cindy, arrived a few days before the wedding, in the wake of winter's first snow. We didn't worry too much about the snow since the first winter weather storms seldom stay for long in our area. Jeff knew Cindy belonged the moment he and Bell met her at the airport.

The banter started when Jeff saw Cindy's large suitcase, packed for only a four-day visit. As he hoisted her case into the trunk, he queried in his robust teasing banter, "How long are you planning to stay?"

She laughed and replied, "Oh, just a month."

Jeff, Bell and Cindy chatted and baited each other all the way home from the airport. The three of them burst into the house on the music of their laughter and I felt instant relief.

Cindy and I connected right away, too, and I enjoyed getting to know this member of Bell's family—this soon-to-be member of my family. We delighted in the retelling of both sides of the romance story between Isabel and Ed.

I knew for certain the two families would knit together quickly when our youngest daughter schemed with Cindy to decorate a local farmer's tractor so the wedding couple could go to the church in country style.

Our earlier lack of concern about the change in the weather soon turned to prayers for reprieve as that first skiff of snow Cindy had flown in on turned into the largest accumulation of snow on record for years.

On December seventh, my husband drove his four-wheel-drive pick-up truck through four-foot drifts to get the wedding cake. Despite the winter blast, guests came from all over the community and from several counties. Phone calls of congratulations came from the east coast for those who waited to welcome the couple in Bedford and Halifax.

The hour came and Dad and Bell, dressed in their finery, scrambled up into the tractor like two eager 16-year-olds. The decorated tractor now boasted Christmas lights and a sign which read "Ed and Isabel's Wedding Chariot." Our neighbour's son-in-law agreed to drive the tractor, so the three of them chugged out the drive and down the road to the church where the crowd of spectators eagerly waited to watch these two octogenarians become one. Jeff and I followed in Dad's car and our van.

I grinned as the two of them quickly hopped off the tractor, and we all hustled out of the storm and into the warmth of the crowded church.

Tears stung and I blinked hard as the bride and groom marched the length of the aisle, backs straight and heads held high. Their quiet vows drifted to the corners of the building amidst a crowd of beaming smiles. I think all of us there that day realized in those moments that love is truly not a respecter of persons or of age. The blushing couple's heartfelt kiss was accompanied by an enthusiastic round of applause. The room sizzled with emotion. Love, happiness, and hope swirled in a dance of abandonment as the years faded from my dad's and step-mom's faces, and we saw the youthful embrace of two hearts.

At the reception afterward, they visited among us like the town's royal couple they had become, though bashful grins betrayed their eagerness to be away. The sense of wonder lingered long after they disappeared into the snowy night, leaving us to ponder the beautiful thing to which we had been witnesses. The thought that life goes on took firm root in our hearts, and left us content as we worked together to remove the flowers and food and return the church to its day-to-day decor.

As the Christmas season approached, Bell settled into her life in the apartment next to our home and seemed content to remain there. But Dad had other ideas. One day he shared them with me.

"You kids are all grown and doing fine. Would you be okay with Bell and me living in Bedford?"

Once more, I found myself in silent rhetorical debate. I'd already lost one parent. I wasn't sure about losing another. But what could I say? Did I have the right to deny them the joy of stepping out into a new life together?

"Airplanes fly east every day." Jeff's pragmatic reply set my mind at ease.

My siblings agreed, so we gave them our blessings and they packed up what they needed and headed east to settle into Bell's apartment in Nova Scotia.

The following months were filled with family visits, happy phone calls, and the lingering awareness that Dad was still losing weight. In candid conversations, Bell told us of her struggle to get more calories into his diet. The worry coloured her words—and mine. She shared that he had been having fluid removed from his lungs to keep a persistent cough under control. Dad waved it off and praised his bride for her loving concern and her great care of him.

Surgery for an unusual growth in Dad's small bowel brought them back to Southern Ontario a few short months after their move. All went well and they soon returned to Nova Scotia and their new life together. The Halifax wedding party planning kicked up a notch, and this time we went east to celebrate.

All of us were startled by Dad's frailty. He shuffled where only short months ago he had marched. The face that carried a beaming

  A Taste of Hot Apple Cider

smile was gaunt and pasty-coloured. Bell and I exchanged worried glances as I hugged my dad.

They went through their wedding vows again, this time in the warmth of spring sunshine. We lingered for a few days, enjoying their shared attention, smiling at their deep love for one another. Too soon our flight time came and Jeff and I jetted back to our Ontario home and the summer ahead.

Then came the phone call. It was the end of August—just after the anniversary of their first phone call. Cindy was calling this time. "Dad's in the hospital," she said. "He was unable to catch his breath so Mom called the ambulance. The doctor said he thinks he'll only last a few days. They aren't saying what it is exactly but we think it might be cancer. I'm sorry, but the doctors said for you to come as soon as you can."

I thanked her for letting us know and hung up. Cancer, the same villain that had stolen our mother, now stalked our father. Numbness settled over me as her words jolted me to the core. A numbness that didn't leave until after I'd dialed through the list of family members who needed to know. Then the feelings came. The twist in the heart. The silent scream—*Not again!*

Taking a deep breath, I went to pack my suitcase. I pondered the oddities of life. Too often, the flame that burns brightest burns for the shortest time.

Four days of life remained from the moment Dad entered the hospital to the moment he flew to his eternal home. Four heartbreaking and beautiful days filled with love in action. Our stepfamily offered us their homes, their hugs, and their tears. We cried together and we laughed together. We dragged the few joint family memories into the sunshine to be examined and treasured. We shared memories from our separate histories. We talked about our mother and our step-siblings talked about their father, and we marvelled at how our two families had melded together so well in such a short time.

As Dad faded into the arms of his Saviour, we learned the real lessons of love. What Dad and Bell shared in their brief days together wasn't an infatuation between two seniors desperate to fill the void of loneliness. No. The two had joined souls under the blessing of their Creator—and joined their families, too. In that year as these two souls came together, I witnessed joy, contentment, selflessness, patience, mercy, generosity, compassion, and graciousness in their fullest measure. In that brief time—just over a year—while I watched the love of two eighty-two-year-olds sprout, grow and burst out into the most glorious blooming, I learned a profound truth. That love has no limits. That no matter how far along the path of life a soul has journeyed, it's never too old to be cradled in the arms of love.

Something to Crow About

Nonfiction

David Kitz

If you asked me if I like birds, without hesitation I would answer, "Yes." If you asked me if I like crows, the quick answer would be, "Not so much."

I suppose it's their voice that irritates me the most. They can't seem to hit the right note. It's their early morning cawing that drives me insane. There's nothing quite as irritating as a crow's relentless caw near your window as you try to get that well-earned hour of extra sleep on a Saturday morning.

I'm convinced someone should invent a beak muzzle for crows. For humanitarian reasons, the muzzle should be designed to allow crows to peck their food and eat normally, but it should be instantly activated the moment they tried to caw.

Surely with all the recent improvements in technology such a device is possible. With the right marketing team I'm sure millions of these devices would be sold. Think for a moment what the ShamWow® guy could do with a beak muzzle!

And consider the prestige. The inventor of a beak muzzle for crows would undoubtedly be awarded the Nobel Prize for Peace— Saturday morning peace. Can there be a higher honour?

But a few years back, I had a dramatic change of heart.

It all started on a lazy Saturday afternoon in the summer. I was sitting in my living room watching a different flock of squawky birds—the Toronto Blue Jays. As I recall, those birds were in a tense match with their rivals the New York Yankees.

Suddenly, KA-BANG! The whole house shook.

My wife came running into the living room shouting, "What happened?"

After a moment of stunned silence, I replied, "I have no idea."

"Well, something hit the house," she insisted.

"I think it hit the front window."

Together we rushed over to our living room picture window. The window itself looked fine. But there on our front lawn lay a crumpled heap of black feathers.

I slipped on my shoes and headed out for a closer look. Sure enough, it was a big crow. The afflicted bird didn't struggle to escape as I approached. He was in no condition to do so. His left wing rested in a splayed-wide state on the grass, while the other wing was tilted up awkwardly, but held close to the body. His head and neck were skewed grotesquely to one side.

I crouched down for a better look. That's when our eyes met.

Until that moment in my mind I had been saying, *Oh good, I'll be rid of one of these pesky nuisances. And if he isn't dead, out of mercy I'll finish him off and bury him in the backyard.*

But his eyes said something quite different.

He was still alive, and he clearly fixed his right eye on me. At the same time, his beak hung open as he frantically gasped for air. With each gulp he seemed to be saying, *Mercy! Mercy! I didn't mean to collide with your window. Mercy!*

We communed eye to eye like that for a few seconds. Then I repented of my murderous thoughts. I said a silent prayer of good health for my hapless feathered friend, stood up, and walked back into the house.

I discussed the state of my fallen comrade with Karen. After considering all the options, we both agreed it was best to leave the crow exactly where he was. Perhaps he was just winded and would recover—a rather unlikely prospect, I thought. But there was no harm in waiting.

I resumed watching those other birds—the Blue Jays. After a particularly tense inning of play, I got up to check on the casualty in the front yard. The crow was gone. I walked out to the spot where he once lay to confirm his disappearance. I looked around the area. No sign of him.

As I re-entered our home I had a smile on my face. I felt strangely happy that the bird had made good his escape without any intervention on my part.

I considered this event to be unusual, but not particularly impactful—except for the crow. And it certainly didn't change my opinion about crows. But the story doesn't end there.

About ten days later, early in the morning, I found myself standing on my front lawn at about the same place where my fallen friend had landed. I was deep in thought—but not about crows and their place in the world. Rather, I was considering that great esoteric question common to man. Can I put off cutting the lawn for another day, or in the great scheme of things should I tackle this chore today?

Suddenly a crow interrupted my contemplation. He fluttered down from a large maple in my neighbour's yard and landed on the front porch. From there he scooted closer onto my driveway. Then this audacious crow walked over to me on my front lawn.

I had never been approached by a crow before. I felt quite uncertain how I should respond. To be blunt, I was thunderstruck.

He, on the other hand, seemed completely at ease. He stopped about a metre from me. Then he looked me over as only a crow can do, cocking his head first to one side, then the other. For a second time, our eyes met. That's when he began to speak, not with his squawky, annoying voice, but with his eyes. Here's what I heard him say—mind to mind:

Sorry for dive bombing your house the other day. That was dumb of me.

Your mercy is appreciated. Thanks for praying for me.

As you can see, I'm fine now.

And with that said, he turned abruptly, flapped his wings a few times, and ascended to his lofty perch in my neighbour's maple tree.

As for me, I returned to my house a humble man.

Since that day, I've thought a good deal about my interaction with that crow. Skeptics might well doubt the truth of my account. Can I prove that the crow that walked up to me was the same crow

that collided with my window? No, I can't. I can't distinguish one crow from another. I can't even tell if the crow I encountered was male or female. But I do know that researchers have found that crows have keen skills of human recognition and recall. Furthermore, I've read and heard countless stories that highlight the intelligence of these birds.

Accuse me of putting words in a bird's beak if you like, but I believe that bird descended to my level and walked over to me with the express purpose of communicating with me in the best way he (or she) could. And he succeeded in his mission.

The Gospel of Luke records the account of Jesus healing ten lepers (Luke 17:11-19), but only one of them returning to give thanks. I showed mercy to one crow and he returned to express thanks. Which is the superior species?

About five-thirty this morning I awoke to the cawing of a crow. And you know something? For me that bird hit all the right notes. I appreciate getting love notes—thank you notes—even from a crow.

Desperate Missionary in Trouble with the Law

Nonfiction

Don Ranney, MD

I'd just finished a sumptuous South Indian breakfast. As the last of my coffee trickled down my throat, there was a knock at the front screen door.

"Telegram for you, Doctor." A man in shabby clothing with a rough turban on his head—really just a cloth wrapped around it—handed me a note. He placed his palms together, bowed slightly and left.

It was January, 1972. I'd been Chief Surgeon at the Schieffelin Leprosy Research Sanatorium[1] in Karigiri, Tamil Nadu, near Vellore in South India, for two years. This was the first time anyone had sent me a telegram. Not sure whether to be nervous or excited, I tore open the envelope.

DAD DIED. HEART ATTACK. FUNERAL FRIDAY.

Not Dad. No! He was so strong and healthy—never sick. It couldn't be true.

I sat there for a few minutes, my mind whirling. Intellectually, I knew I was in shock and that it would be very difficult, if not impossible for me to get there in time for the funeral. But I also knew that I had to see him in his coffin. Only then could I accept that he had truly passed away. Irrational, maybe, but I had to go home in order to have closure. And there was no time to waste.

I picked up my phone and contacted the hospital switchboard.

"I just received news my father died."

"Yes, Doctor. I sent you telegram, just arrived."

"Send a reply: Coming home."

"Yes, Doctor. As soon as Superintendent authorizes."

"No, send it now. This is urgent."

"Not possible. Hospital policy."

I slammed the phone down and began to think. Direct flights to Canada go from Bombay. I'd flown from Bombay last year en route to a training course in Ethiopia. I knew the flight from Madras to Bombay[2] leaves at six-thirty p.m. daily. I had to be on that flight. *Madras is roughly 140 kilometers from here, about a three-hour drive,* I thought. *Assuming all goes well. But first, I need a ticket for the flight to Bombay.*

Last year, I'd bought a ticket from the manager of the Trans World Airlines (TWA) Office in Madras and developed a good relationship with him. Foreign money tends to be worth more, so anyone who buys a ticket in India with money from his own overseas bank account finds everyone loves him. *I'll ask the manager of the TWA offices to get me a ticket, and pay him when I get there. No problem. But can I get to Madras in time to catch the flight?*

In an emergency, a surgeon's mind can think at the speed of a hurricane. Leaving India wasn't just a matter of having an airplane ticket. Not for a missionary who wanted to return. There were many documents to obtain and places to go—and barely any time to do it. I had to:

- Provide evidence all income taxes due had been paid.

- Get a letter of good conduct from the local Chief of Police—this takes two weeks! A policeman cycles around the district asking people if the missionary has done any bad deeds, hurt anyone, owed money, etc. He then hands a handwritten report to the Chief.

- Take both to The District Collector for Tamil Nadu in nearby Vellore, who will write a letter to authorize my departure. A District Collector is the chief administrative and revenue officer of an Indian district. Appointments take twenty-four hours to obtain.

- Visit the Indian Government's Secretary of State for Tamil Nadu with this letter and obtain a visa to re-enter India. Canadians did not typically require a visa, but all missionaries were considered to be felons until proven otherwise. After all, our professed role was to subvert the thinking of good Hindus and convert them to Christianity. It didn't matter in official circles that I was a surgeon doing reconstructive surgery on leprosy patients most Indian doctors refused to help. I was loved by all—but a suspicious person in the eyes of the government.

- Buy a return ticket to fly from Madras, India to Toronto, Canada.

I decided to just skip the first two, barge in unannounced to see the District Collector and get him to tell me how I could see the Secretary of State. As I thought furiously through all this, anyone watching might have seen steam coming out of my ears.

I'd met the District Collector a week before when he visited our hospital for a "function" to commemorate a milestone in the life of our institution. Each Department Head made a little speech; then we ate a delicious meal. People shook hands or gave the Indian palms-together-slight-bow and we departed.

It always irritated me that although everyone knew English, many chose to speak in their "native" tongue—Tamil, Malayalam, Hindi or whatever. To secretly express my displeasure, when my time came, I said, "*Je suis Canadien. Je ne parle pas français.* So I'll speak in English." Then I gave my short speech. This unwittingly gave me an advantage. This official would remember me.

I had the hospital driver take me to the District Collector's house, the site of his office. Social customs demanded a secretary could not have an office in his employer's house. He worked in a tent in the driveway and from it he told me, "He is unavailable today." I walked past him and knocked on the door of the house.

The District Collector warmly invited me in, saying, "I remember you. Aren't you the doctor who speaks French?" To this day, I don't know whether he was joking at my expense or being genuinely friendly.

After I explained my situation, he said, "Of course, the son must be at his father's funeral. I will make it happen."

Later I recalled the Hindu belief that if a son doesn't light his father's funeral pyre there is no hope of him entering Nirvana.

Quickly, he wrote a letter for me to take to the Secretary of State, who was the Representative of the State of Tamil Nadu to the Government of India.

"On the envelope," he said, "I've written his home address in Madras. He should be there after work at six p.m. He lives just beside the airport. I shall phone to tell him you are coming and ask him to bring home his visa stamp for your passport."

I thanked him profusely, bowed and walked back to the hospital car. As I passed the Collector's assistant, he scowled at me. Inwardly, I smiled.

When I got back to my home, it was ten-thirty, and I still didn't have a ticket for the plane that evening.

I located the phone number of the TWA main office in Madras and asked the telephone operator to connect me.

"Cost much money," he said. "Will ask Superintendent."

"Did you send the telegram?"

"Oh yes. Long time ago."

I sighed. "Please connect me with the operating room."

While my wife Julia packed two suitcases, I talked with the operating room head nurse.

"I have to go to Canada today—"

"Yes, I know, sir. Your father died. I have informed Dr. Thomson and cancelled the two more complicated operations he tells me that he is not qualified to do. He said he would be happy to cover for you in your absence, and also he wishes you a safe trip."

"Thank you, Brother[3] Arumagam. I wish the rest of this hospital was as efficient as you and the local information network. I'll be back soon. *Poitu Varen.*[4]" I put down the phone; it rang immediately. I picked it up, hoping it was my call to Madras. Instead, it was Dr. Kurian, Hospital Superintendent. "I understand your concern about your father's sudden death," he said. "But you have a job to do here. Can Thomson fill in for you?"

"I'm certain of that, and he's agreed to do it."

"All right, I'll book a long distance call to TWA head office in Madras. But it could take four hours to get through. We don't have those fancy long distance telephone wires you have in Canada."

  A Taste of Hot Apple Cider

By noon I was pacing the floor. An idea sprang like a Bengal tiger into my head. *I'll leave at one p.m.—no later, and get the Superintendent to order the ticket.*

I phoned Dr. Kurian to ask him if he would handle the long distance call when it came through, and have the airline company manager meet me at the airport with the ticket.

"I'll talk to him," he said. "But you shall be responsible for the cost of the flight. I can only provide you with compassionate leave and a car to the airport. I'll send a car to collect you after lunch. You'll have to return from Madras yourself by train. Leprosy Mission Head Office in London should cover the cost of all travel in India, but flying to Canada will not be covered without prior approval; and that cannot happen now."

Oow! I'd forgotten about the money issue. *Wait! I still have a Canadian bank account. I'll write a cheque on it.*

At one-thirty, a rambling old jalopy pulled up to my front door. "Car for you, Doctor," the driver said.

I threw my two suitcases in the back seat, kissed Julia goodbye, and climbed in beside the driver. We rumbled off down the road, a cloud of dust marking our trail.

After half an hour, I looked at the speedometer. We were travelling less than forty miles per hour. At this rate, I'd miss my flight.

"We must go faster, Babu," I said. "At least fifty miles an hour in order to catch the plane."

"Can't go more than forty. Superintendent said. Car not good."

"Well if you go fifty miles an hour going there, and thirty back, that's an average of forty, isn't it?"

Babu frowned, then smiled. "Okay, Doctor. We go fifty."

A breeze from the window dried the sweat on my forehead as we sped along. We met the usual herd of buffaloes going down the road and twice had to move off the road to avoid being run down by large trucks going in the opposite direction. But, before five p.m., we'd reached Madras Airport and found the politician's house, a modest dwelling overlooking the airport's main departure runway.

I eagerly ascended the front steps and introduced myself to the woman who came to the door. She invited me in to wait for him. She said he was expected on the next flight from Delhi where he'd been to a "function" commemorating the Constitution of India coming into force in 1950 to replace the old British Government of India Act.

"Isn't Republic Day tomorrow?" I asked.

"Yes," she replied. "That is when he must be here to officially unfurl the national flag in front of all the people."

I smiled, bowed slightly, and thanked her with my palms together. I glanced at my watch. *Almost five. I hope he gets here soon.*

By six p.m., I felt a knot in my stomach. My plane was scheduled to leave at six-thirty.

At ten past six, a short bald-headed man walked in the door. As he saw me, his eyes widened. "Oh, you must be the missionary from Vellore. I completely forgot! We had a big party in Delhi after finalizing all the plans for tomorrow. Sit down and hand me your passport."

I did so, as he rustled through his large brief case. "Not here. I do not have the official visa stamp. No problem. I shall copy out the old one."

Meticulously, he wrote on another page the contents of my old visa, stamped it with his personal stamp, signed it and wrote the date. Handing it to me, he smiled, then said with some alarm, "Your plane leaves in five minutes. I think you will miss it."

"No worry, sir. I've taken it several times before. The six-thirty plane never leaves until seven p.m." With that, I bowed slightly, and hurried to the car.

"To the airport, quickly," I told Babu.

After Babu dropped me off and headed home, presumably at thirty miles an hour, I entered the airport and walked all around but saw no one who looked like the manager of the TWA offices, who should be there with my ticket.

I enquired at the Indian Airlines desk. They knew him, but said he'd not been seen there that day.

Stranded. What to do? I didn't even have his phone number at his office in Madras. And it was too late for him to get to the airport in time even if I did have his number. I'd left with the understanding that my Superintendent would ask him to meet me with a ticket. What had gone wrong?

At ten minutes before seven, I heard the last call for the flight to Bombay, and sadly watched as the rolling staircase was moved away from the door. Sharp at seven p.m., the six-thirty flight took off. I sat down and pondered my impossible future. The next flight was at six-thirty the following evening. No matter what I did, I'd miss the funeral. And I didn't even have a ride back to my hospital.

"Call for Doctor Ranney, call for Doctor Ranney," a voice on the loudspeaker said. At the Indian Airlines counter, a smiling female clerk handed me the phone.

"Hello, Doctor Ranney. I've been waiting for you in my office since five p.m. You wanted a ticket. What happened?"

I groaned. "The Hospital Superintendent put through the call to you for me while I drove here. I'd asked him to ask you if you could please meet me at the airport because I didn't have time to go into the city to pick up the ticket. But I guess he was too polite to make such a suggestion. Now I don't know what to do. The airplane has gone."

"I have a solution. The Superintendent told me you need to get to Toronto, Canada. I can get you there through the ten p.m. flight to Delhi, which I'm taking myself. I'll just bump one of the Madras State Members of Parliament going there for the three-day Republic Day celebration. He can go next year."

My heart began thumping. "You'd do that for me? How can I repay you?"

"Paying for the return ticket to Toronto is enough. I have great respect for you foreign surgeons who come here to help the poorest of the poor. I'm doing this to thank you."

Eight hours later, we approached the landing strip in London, England. I smiled and thanked God for taking care of me.

Then a message came over the speaker. "Attention, all wishing to travel to Canada. The Air Controller's Union in Canada is on strike and there are no flights to or from Canada. However, if you already made arrangements to go there, we will, at no extra charge, put you on a plane to Boston or New York, USA, via Dublin. Your baggage will be forwarded automatically. DO NOT—I repeat—DO NOT collect your baggage, but go directly to South Terminal and embark on the flight to Dublin. It leaves thirty-five minutes after we land."

Oh, my.

That wasn't my only problem. I'd paid for my ticket with a personal cheque from my old Canadian bank account, but I didn't know if there was any money in it.

I thought of something else, and opened my passport to look at the hand written visa in it. The Indian Government's Secretary of State for Tamil Nadu had quite correctly copied the phrase, "This visa is valid as long as the passport is valid."

With a sinking feeling, I looked at the first page of my passport. As I feared, the passport had expired. I was in very deep trouble.

Into my head sprang the Scripture: "The Lord is my Shepherd, I shall not want." Really? "Yea, though I walk through the valley of the shadow of death, I will fear no evil; for Thou art with me…"[5] *Well,* I thought, *it isn't that bad…yet.* I began to hope.

As I walked into London's Gatwick airport, a chill ran down my spine. Not fear this time, but the cold temperature. In the land I'd left it was about 80 degrees Fahrenheit (25.5 Celsius). In my shorts and T-shirt, the "normal" indoor temperature of the airport reception hall, about 68 degrees Fahrenheit, was frigid.

Even if I'd been able to find my luggage, there was no time to get a sweater. I headed straight for South Terminal and the gate to board for Dublin. There were about fifteen of us. An attendant came from nowhere, unlocked the door, handed us boarding passes, and let us on the plane. Once seated, I snuggled up in a blanket.

It was a short flight with time only for a snack. An attendant came down the aisle with passes for flights to either Boston or New York. The Boston flight went on to Detroit, so I took that one. The stopover in Dublin would only be forty-five minutes, so still no chance to get near our luggage. Surely I could get a sweater out of my suitcase in Detroit. This thought warmed my heart, but not my body.

All hope for warm clothes vanished when we landed in Detroit. Our luggage had been transferred to a bus that would take us to Toronto. I shivered in a draughty hangar for forty-five minutes while we waited for that bus to collect us.

Before going to India, people told me to expect culture shock. But shock is always something you don't expect. I'd studied the country and its people. I was a trained anthropologist as well as a surgeon, so I was prepared for India and felt very little culture shock.

On arriving at the Toronto airport, however, this "dude" with shoulder length blonde hair and a face that otherwise looked like my brother Ken approached me. He spoke. It was Ken, a family doctor who had always been pretty conventional. For the first time in my life—I was truly in shock!

Canada had undergone a cultural revolution in the late sixties/early seventies that had completely bypassed me. Now I was in Canada, my home, but really, I was in a foreign culture I used to call home.

The funeral on Saturday—postponed by a day to allow me to be there—was a celebration of my dad's life, long before they used that term. But what else could it be for a man who had served God all his adult life? He co-founded Dawes Road Gospel Church, not only served as Chairman of the Board and Sunday School Superintendent, but with the help of a few others had physically built the structure. This congregation of about fifty people partially supported eleven missionaries. My wife and I were two of them.

In fact, I often felt that I was but an extension of my dad's life. Maybe that was why I had such difficulty believing he had passed away.

On Sunday, I was asked to speak to the church about our work. The minister took up a "free-will" offering in addition to the regular offering. These "saints," for I must call them that, contributed exactly enough to cover the cost of my flight.

At the bank the next day, I learned there had only been ten dollars in the account. Fortunately, the cheque for the air ticket had not yet come through. I quickly deposited the money the congregation had given me, worrying that the cheque might come in the door by courier before I could complete the transaction.

Truly the Lord is my Shepherd, I thought. *He restores my soul— and my bank account!*

Now I had to get a new passport. My return flight left on Saturday morning. Passports used to come from Ottawa, but now I could apply in Toronto, so to the subway I went.

No problem, the clerk in the Toronto Passport office told me. "You'll have your passport in a week at the most."

"A week?" I said. "My ticket says I must fly Saturday."

"I'll mark it 'Expedite.' You might get it by Friday."

Something more to worry about—or pray about. *This whole event has been a series of miracles. Lord, we need one more please. No two! I also need a visa to re-enter India as a missionary.*

The passport arrived late on Friday. There was no time for me to get a visa.

Early the next morning, I said goodbye to friends and family, trusting God that somehow I would be allowed into India to "corrupt the minds of good Hindus and turn them into Christians." I reflected on this idea, and the fact that I rarely had a chance to preach in India anyway. I wasn't a "sower of the seed—the Word of God," but as a surgeon you could say I fertilized the soil. Well, in the eyes of the government I was as guilty as the others—an accomplice.

Yet another miracle happened without my even praying about it. When I got to the airport, I discovered that the air controllers' strike was over. I could fly Air Canada directly to Bombay with only a refuelling stop in London.

On landing at Bombay airport, after collecting my two suitcases, I hesitated. There were two lines in front of me: a long one in front of the sign that read "Foreigners with Visa," and a much more quickly processed short one in front of a sign that read, "No Visa Required."

Reluctantly, I moved toward the longer line.

As I did so, a well-dressed official came up to me, saw I was holding a Canadian passport and smiled with a face that resembled a sunrise. "Don't go there," he said. "You are a Canadian. You are welcome here. Come in without a visa—no problem."

"B-but I'm a—"

"You are a Canadian. That is all that matters. Come, come, I will lead the way."

Sweat dripped from my forehead as I made my way through. It seemed to be hotter than I remembered. God had worked yet another miracle.

But one more problem remained. During the next few days I had to visit the Chief of Police and the Government Tax Office to apologize for bypassing them in my rush to go home.

But each one said much the same. "We understand. A son must go home when his father dies. How else can his father reach Nirvana?"

Oh, I love these Hindus. They are such wonderfully kind people!

1. Now called Schieffelin Institute of Health—Research and Leprosy Centre

2. Madras is now called Chennai and Bombay, Mumbai.

3. In India, male nurses are called "Brother," female ones "Sister."

4. *Poitu Varen* is a Tamil word meaning "Going I will come."

5. Psalm 23:4, King James Version

A Time to Have Tea

Nonfiction

Vilma Blenman

It's Monday of week three of my radiation treatments following two surgeries for breast cancer. I'm already tired of the treks to Sunnybrook Hospital, tired of arranging the weekly schedule of daily rides: pick up, drop off, half day at work or whole day, or not at all, drive myself and deal with parking at the hospital or have someone drive me, either from work or from home. And if I drive first to work, then what happens to the car if someone drives me to treatment? All options have to be revisited daily because the schedule changes daily, and my energy levels ebb and flow daily with the tides.

The oncologist and the nurses told me I'd start to feel fatigue, and to adjust my schedule accordingly, but except for a week off following each surgery, and two weeks preceding the radiation treatments, I've kept up a normal pace at home and at work. Cancer or no cancer, I'm still mother, wife, teacher, and counsellor to at-risk teens. But something is changing in my body and soul. I usually begin the week rested and grounded, but not today.

I close my eyes, remembering last Thursday. It was horrible. What was I thinking even leaving the house in that terrible snow storm? I still feel the car dancing on the icy road, still feel my hands gripping the cold wheel, still feel my jellied left foot pumping the brakes in a panic, trying to stay in control. It could have been so bad. It's a miracle I made it home safely.

Today, my husband drives me to work. As I take the passenger seat, relief floods me. I won't have to make decisions every minute about lane changes, when to speed up, when to slow down. These details never used to bother me, but now I feel distress even thinking about them. One of the women from the library small group at my church offered to pick me up and drive me to the hospital for my two p.m. radiation therapy appointment. She'll wait for me and drive me home after. When she offered, I almost told her not to bother. I'm so glad I held my tongue.

When I walk into the brown-brick high school at 8:32, BJ[1] is sitting in the hallway outside the library doors as usual. He gets up and follows me into Support Room, a self-contained room located just inside the library's steel double doors. But before I can even take my coat off, another student walks in. "Can I print something?"

"Sure," I say. If only all requests were that simple.

I look over at BJ standing in a corner. His lips are pursed. His shoulders sag and his lowered chin reaches towards his chest.

"Miss, can I talk to you?"

"Yeah. I'll be right with you."

I take off my coat and hang it up, put my lunch bag in the fridge, then beckon for BJ to follow me into the adjoining counselling room, away from the common open area consisting of computers, study carrels, and a couch. When BJ looks up, I can see the woes spilling out of his eyes.

Support Room, where I work each weekday from eight forty-five a.m. to four p.m., functions as an informal drop-in and a formal referral counselling space for at-risk teens who need socio-emotional and academic support.

In other words, we deal with anything from anger management counselling to coping with depression, anxiety or bullying, to the classic procrastination problem when the student finally declares: "I need help with this assignment due like last week and I've been skipping class until it's done."

Part of the larger Guidance and Student Success Department in our high school, the staff in Support Room consists of a certified Child and Youth Worker and me, an English teacher with counselling credentials. Students can see either or both of us, together or separately. BJ is equally comfortable talking to either of us, but I've been missing days because of surgery and radiation treatments so I feel less up-to-date on BJ's emotional needs than normal. Ms. Lyle, my co-worker, would be more aware, but she's not in yet, and I'm here.

Ms. Lyle is an amazing youth worker. She's young, vivacious and so teen savvy, aware of the latest music, the latest TV shows, the latest celebrity news. She's deeply empathic, yet firmly no-nonsense, knowing when to say, "Stop this and smarten up" and when to say, "I hear your hurt. How can I help you?" I wish she were here now.

BJ follows me into the counselling room, closes the door, and slumps into one of the two blue-tweed chairs positioned to face each other. I go to my desk and turn on the banker's lamp that I brought from home some years ago to add more light and warmth to the room. Turning on the lamp is part of my morning ritual. A yellow glow spreads through the room, rays reaching across to the bright orange wall, and up the posters that proclaim the ways of success. The light is instant comfort. I deposit my little brown bag with the hospital gowns on the table in the corner; make the two piles on my desk one neat stack, then move back towards the other side of the room and sit in the second blue chair. Facing BJ, I suddenly realize I'm too tense, too scattered. I remind myself to breathe. I become present. I wait for him to begin.

"She blocked my number on the weekend. Then when I finally got to talk to her on Facebook and I ask her why, she said, 'Because I'm no good. I've been trying to tell you to stay away because I'm not worth it.'"

"Oh dear. That's hard. Hard on you, BJ. I'm so sorry." I feel as if there's a hurricane coming, as if I need to get myself away and get others out of the eye of the storm. But with teens it's always hurricane season. So I sit quietly and remind myself that this is the stuff of teen angst. It's the latest installment in the BJ and Moira saga of tragic-doomed-to-fail love story. Moira is depressed and suicidal. BJ used to be suicidal, but no longer. Still anxious, though.

I ask him how this makes him feel. I'm worried about the effect of this turbulence on him.

"I don't know. I'm just so upset. I was in a really good space, I haven't cut for over fifty days and counting."

"Hmmm, "I say, nodding, letting him know I hear him.

From earlier conversations with BJ and Ms. Lyle, I gather that BJ believes he truly understands Moira and thinks he can save her.

Moira tells him she wants to be saved, but I'm not so sure she does. Or maybe she does, but not by him. By some other knight. But of course she won't tell him that. Now he's tortured by the possibility of her harming herself, permanently.

Ms. Lyle and I know Moira. We worry about her, too. Ms. Lyle sees Moira on a daily basis, lets her come and sit next to her and talk her heart out. In addition, there are several other professional caregivers inside and outside the school who work with Moira to monitor her mental health for safety and other concerns. BJ has unofficially added his name as primary caregiver.

After a long silence, BJ says, "I think she's trying to push me away so she can justify that no one loves her, that life is not worth living. I don't know what to do." He raises his palms, the fingers splayed as if counting them is his next task.

I let the silence be, allowing him to hear himself. Then I say, "Space is what she seems to be asking from you. Maybe space is a good thing."

"I know." His new blue bangs fall forward as he lowers his blond head into his shaking hands. "But I don't want to lose her. I can't lose her," he says in a muffled voice.

He wants to save her from herself. I want to save him from her. From his pointless sacrificial offering of love. But I know I can't. I've told him several times that his own self-care, his own self-preservation, has to be his focus now.

"Look after you," I say to BJ as he grabs a tissue, shoulders his knapsack, and slowly walks to the door.

I realize the irony of my last words.

And what about me? I wonder. *What about my self-preservation?*

Self-care is something I teach. But now I want to by-pass it for myself. I just want to get back to normal. *When, how, do I get back to normal? Is there normal after cancer?*

The rest of the morning at work is normal. Ms. Lyle arrives. The morning bells ring. Chattering crowds move through the halls. "O Canada" plays on the school's PA system. Classes begin. After I update Ms. Lyle on BJ, I attend to an array of student needs. I answer emails, edit a student's resume as promised and track down two students to follow up at teachers' requests. At mid-morning, I go into the common room to our self-serve tea area by the microwave and turn on the kettle to boil water.

Then I meet with Ms. Lyle to plan a mediation for after lunch. "The Fab Five again?" I say, when Ms. Lyle tells me who the mediation is with.

"Yeah, but not the whole group. Something happened. I don't know what, but the group has split into two."

The mediation, requested by one of our vice-principals, is between two Grade nine girls who wield much power in the school. Both were originally part of the Fabulous Five, a group of four popular girls and one not so popular boy who became their loyal follower and bodyguard. The group manages to roam the halls en masse by texting to co-ordinate bathroom breaks from their various classes. They stage drama inside and outside classrooms; they bully girls, and generally create full-time jobs for the vice-principals, their disciplinary visits to the office are so regular.

I shut my eyes briefly. *Here comes another hurricane,* I tell myself. I feel too tired to run, too tired to grab people and pull them along.

Ms. Lyle's voice pulls me back to the room as we sum up the situation. Each group is now headed by one of the most popular and the meanest of the mean girls. The boy was apparently forced to choose a group, and choose he did. We'd be meeting with two intractable heads of state.

Facilitating mediations between feuding students is a normal enough part of our work in Support Room. Both Ms. Lyle and I are trained in conflict resolution strategies.

After a fight or a potential fight, the vice-principals generally refer students for a mediation session in which each party gets to air grievances individually "far from the madding crowd." After we coach each one on how to deliver an "I Message," we bring them together so they can collectively devise a plan for peaceful co-existence within the school. Then both parties sign a contract they think is realistic to keep.

It's a proven strategy for reducing reoccurrence of the conflict. Parents may also request mediation. Sometimes students request mediation if they can't resolve an issue by themselves. Oddly enough, this is one of those self-referrals, after the girls had each seen the vice-principal.

"They each say they want to make peace," the VP reports to us in her pre-mediation briefing. *As if they are emissaries of warring countries,* I think.

Ms. Lyle and I both know peace is probably not the girls' primary motive. More likely, each wants information from the other and this is a safe way to get it.

Since Support Room functions as a drop-in at lunch time, I tend to work through lunch. Today is no different. Many students show up, some of whom I've been meaning to see for various reasons.

When the end-of-lunch bell rings, we call down each girl and begin the mediation. The individual story-telling part goes smoothly enough, but when they meet, the dialogue drags on and on as we try to untangle the threads of who did what to whom.

"That couldn't be true because Sasha said that you said I started drama again 'cause I was giving you dirty looks in science. I didn't even look at you and your friends the whole time."

"Yeah, but you're the one who posted some message about watch out for big red going down today at McDonald's. I'm the one with red streaks in my hair, so I know you're talking about me."

Back and forth the volley goes, each girl trying to ascertain the other's level of aggression and what concession she can make without giving up her lead girl role. At the end of what seems like a UN negotiations deal they both agree on some things. Finally Ms. Lyle writes up a peace contract that each signs. I feel as if I've aged a decade.

As the girls leave the room, I realize the time. "Oh, no," I say to Ms. Lyle. "I have to go now."

"Go," she says. "I'll update the VP."

I grab the brown paper bag with my blue hospital gowns, withdraw my purse hidden in the filing cabinet and pull my coat off the hook behind the door. Then I run like a madwoman down the hall and out the front doors.

Lily, my volunteer driver, is in her car, waiting in the front of the school, her face carrying a bundle of smiles. I feel exhausted, as if I've just worked two shifts and overtime on an assembly line at GM.

As we drive west down Lawrence Avenue, she listens to me recount my normal Monday morning and afternoon. Her hand is steady on the wheel. She stops gently at red lights, no lurching, no agonizing whether to go through amber lights or not. Every so often she smiles at me, the kind of smile that says, "It's okay. You can rest now."

I tell her that I almost said no to her offer to drive me, but that God is teaching me to accept offers.

Lily looks over at me, her eyes shining in the winter afternoon light. "They are really His offers, aren't they? His gifts to you."

Lily's words quieten me. I sit back, but stay vigilant not to miss the big blue "H" sign signalling the hospital. Suddenly we are there.

"Turn here," I tell Lily. "The parking lot up there on the right is closer to where I go but it's often full."

Fortunately, there's a vacant spot in the Odette Cancer Centre parking lot. Lily parks and we head inside. I'm racing inside, but I'm actually early for my appointment.

As soon as I register at the reception desk, the lead radiation therapist, one of three who look after me, appears to escort me to the familiar room for a date with the big machine.

I undress and put on my blue floral gowns in the familiar change area—Section 13, the cubicle right beside the big red sign that warns of radioactive activity.

In the waiting area, I see the same care-worn faces I've seen for weeks, some young, some not so young, all shades, all shapes and I think of Mom, who once remarked, "Cancer does not discriminate." I wait for my name to be called again.

"There you are," the therapist says. She's always cheery. "We're ready for you. Come on in."

I know the routine. I lie down; I bare my left breast. She adjusts the machine that arches over me and calls out numbers to the other technician therapist who makes adjustments for exactly the right dose of radiation.

  A Taste of Hot Apple Cider

"You look so tired," she says, bending down to position my head. "Are you getting enough rest?"

"I'm taking tomorrow off."

"Do you have to work the rest of the week?"

"The work I do is with students. I feel I need to be there as much as possible. Kids don't schedule a crisis and they don't want to have to tell their story again and again to someone else."

"Isn't there another counsellor available if there's a crisis?"

"I... Well, yes, there is. I'm not indispensable. I know that."

"You have to take care of yourself."

"I know. But I feel I'm being wimpy. All I do is come here and lie down under a machine."

The therapist pauses, looks me in the eye, then speaks, the usual cheer absent from her voice. "Well, if anyone says you're a wimp, ask them if they'd like to try it."

I know she's offering comfort, but I flinch. *That was a bit harsh,* I think.

My mind wanders from planets to people while the machine groans and drones on, doing its own thing. And then, there is silence.

Just as suddenly I'm up checking tomorrow's schedule, dressing, taking my gowns and heading back to Lily in the main waiting room. Soon we're back in the car, heading towards Highway 401.

By the time Lily drops me at home, it's almost three fifteen, nearly time for my fourteen-year-old son to get home from school.

"Who's driving you, tomorrow?" Lily asks.

"Ellen is. Tuesdays work well for her."

Ellen is another of the women in the library small group at our church. The group collects and catalogues books and takes turns signing out books on Sunday mornings, encouraging both kids and adults to use the church library as a resource place. We just started attending the church and I'd signed up for that group at the beginning of September, then discovered the cancer diagnosis that led to surgery by the end of September. I'd sent an email to Ellen, one of the group's organizers, apologizing for missing the meetings. She was one of the first to offer rides to radiation treatment, though I barely knew who she was.

As I enter our kitchen, it dawns on me that I'm hungry. I remember boiling the kettle, but I don't recall making my mid-morning tea. I realize that my lunch is still sitting in the fridge. Lunch time was so busy, and the few times I did think of eating, the microwave was occupied by students heating up soup packets or left over food from Sunday suppers. I sigh. It's not the first time I've left my lunch at work. It won't be the last, either.

I find soup in our fridge, warm it, eat it, then head to bed. It's the only thing I have enough energy to do.

I drag myself up the stairs, holding on to the railing. I feel dizzy. I climb into bed, but I can't sleep. Lying there at that strange rest hour, I try to piece together the day like a detective recon-structing an accident scene. I was only at work for four and a half hours. Nothing unusual happened. So why am I so breathlessly tired?

Just to remind myself, I say out loud, "Remember to tell Ellen that tomorrow's treatment time is changed to eleven a.m."

I wake up suddenly, disoriented. *Why am I in bed?* I lie back, remembering. I must have slept, at least for a few minutes. I smell French fries baking and hear things moving around downstairs.

"Hey, Mom." Josiah bounds into the room. Since our son stopped crawling thirteen years ago, he hasn't walked. He always runs. And leaps.

"I got all my science done."

"Good for you. What was it you were working on?"

"I had to finish writing up a lab." He's looking into my eyes. "Do you want some tea?"

I summon the energy to reply. "Yeah, sure."

"What kind do you want me to make?"

"What's there?" My husband has been doing the grocery shop-ping since my surgery.

"I saw something called Spiced Chai, and there's regular tea, and some mint tea."

The truth is I don't really want tea. Or at least not the tea my son will make from lukewarm water in the kettle. I want my chai, made my way, a variation of true chai from India, a rich black tea made with milk, a combination of spices, and sweetened to perfection. My chai, like most of my recipes, is really an intuitive Caribbean-Canadian combo. First I pour two cups of cold water in my small pot and make a fragrant brew with cinnamon sticks, green cardamom seeds, a few cloves, and two star anise. I let it simmer before I add the chai tea bags and steep exactly five minutes. Then I add some warmed coconut milk, a spoonful or two of maple syrup and sweetened condensed milk. I stir the whole thing to a frothy full flavour and strain it into my favourite mug.

Josiah stands looking down at me in the bed, waiting for my answer.

I vacillate. But I know I want to encourage my son to offer practical compassion to others, so I tell him, "Spiced Chai is good. I'd like that. Thanks."

He hurries off, and I try to get up; then I lie back down.

Rest, you must rest. Take care of you. That's what you tell them in Support Room.

I slide beneath the mound of blankets and blue-and-white cushions, hues of blue all around me.

When I open my eyes again, Josiah is entering the room, cradling tea in a giant mug that looks more like a soup bowl. The very sight of him walking into our bedroom, mug in hand, a big grin on his face, warms me, and chases away the stiff, cold thing in me. I want to weep.

"Mom, is tea supposed to be sweet? I don't even know."

"It doesn't have to be."

"I thought it should be, but I didn't know. I put some dabs of honey in it."

"Dabs of honey sound good," I say. I picture him in the kitchen, coaxing the sticky droplets of honey from the nearly empty plastic bottle, squeezing out the air, willing the honey to come. And likely as not, it sputtered and splattered all over the kitchen counter. I'll probably have to wipe it off when I get up. But I won't think about that… I sit up and push a pillow behind my back.

He gives me the mug. The pure, earthy aroma of spices in the chai surrounds me.

I take a small sip. The tart black tea stabs my taste buds in the middle and along the sides; but before it becomes too much, the sweet honey registers comfort at the tip of my tongue.

"Mmm," I say. "Not bad at all. This is good tea, Josiah. Thanks."

"You're welcome," he says, beaming. He leaves quickly.

I take a deep breath. *Dabs of honey,* I think, recalling his expression. Perhaps that's what makes this unwelcomed journey, this crazy cancer ride, bearable. It's bitter, yes, but along the way there are indeed dabs of honey. I sip and give thanks, suddenly feeling grateful for all the gifts God has given me since the doctor's words to me in September: neighbours and strangers to drive me, flowers to cheer me, frank family talks about life and death, the courage to stare cancer in the face and say, "You don't scare me." And now, in this mellowed moment, chai with honey. I hold tightly the cup of tea as it warms my hands. *If only I weren't so tired,* I think again and again.

And then, in the quiet of the blue room, His words come to me like a lullaby sung from deep inside—a lilting, lifting lullaby that fills the room with melodies of flutes. And the rising notes take me far away from the morning in Support Room, far away from the afternoon at the hospital, far from the impossible to-do lists downstairs and the requests waiting in my unopened email.

This time in your life—it's tea time. A time to have tea. A time to take care of self and soul. A time to accept the gracious help from all the caregivers given to you.

I know I'm in my room, on my bed. But I'm also in a field of tall, waving grass. A warm wind blows. The scent of cinnamon wafts over me. I feel a sense of calm, of peace.

Suddenly the door bursts open and Josiah is back, breathing heavily from his run upstairs. "You okay, Mom?"

"Yeah, sure," I say, bending my wet face toward the empty mug. Then I look up, not caring if he sees the tears. "The tea was so good, Josiah. Exactly what I needed. You can make tea for me any time."

---

1. Most names and some details have been changed to ensure the anonymity of the people in this story.

A Taste of Hot Apple Cider

In His Shoes

Nonfiction

Keturah Harris

During our first decade together, I thought my father could do no wrong. During our next three decades, I was convinced he could do no right. Now, entering our final season together, I realize he could do no better.

I'm walking with my father today. That in itself is *hugely* significant. First of all, it means I had to take a break from my all-consuming work to catch the early afternoon rays of the just-before-spring sunshine. In the past, I would have felt obligated to finish my "to do" list first, but of late I've come to realize that while the work will always be there, my father won't. It's taken me a lifetime of living to finally understand that the things that make life worth living only get noticed when we stop to value the worth of a life.

The other aspect that makes our father-daughter walk so miraculous is that a few short weeks ago (or even a few weeks from now) such an activity would have been neither probable nor even possible. Not only would the icy cold weather have made our pursuit of a neighbourhood promenade ridiculous, but the freezing weather would have had a formidable conspirator in the icy cold hand of death that has become a close and constant companion since my father's cancer diagnosis just last fall.

But today, for a few short moments, the sun is shining enough, the sidewalk is clear enough, and my father's weakened knees are strong enough to support his dramatically shrunken frame, allowing us this special time together.

It's so good to stroll leisurely in the sunshine. Such an unusual pleasure for me, the power-walker, to slow my pace to the speed of my dad's hesitating gait and to really tune in, to literally come alongside and for a magically brief space in time, travel away from the cruelty of illness to a much kinder place of meaningless small talk, juicy gossip, and politically incorrect opinions. To act momentarily as if time was ours to squander and the world was ours to control.

Yes, I notice the shortness of breath, the strained determination, and the awkward need to stop every so often to cough and spit (a parting gift the brutal rounds of chemo left behind). And yes, I hold my breath on more than one occasion as I observe his footsteps falter, and position myself to catch him if he should stumble and fall.

How often in my life has he caught me when I was stumbling and falling? First as my "daddy," that formidable male-figure whom I both adored more than anyone else and feared more than anyone else. My giant daddy, who loomed larger than life, who literally picked me up when I fell down, who sometimes squeezed my hand tightly to keep me moving along the paths of life. My hero daddy, who swooped in and saved me from the sticks and stones that could break my bones and those awful names that hurt me. My talented daddy, who created beautiful furniture from wood frames and carefully taught me my first lessons in fabric and design. My disciplinarian daddy, who wouldn't hesitate to deliver a sharp word in my ears or a hard tap to my bottom when naughtiness got the best of me. My thoughtful daddy, who took the time to make miniature furniture for miniature me in irresistible, tangerine-tufted elegance. Yes, he was always there to catch me when I fell…

That is, until the time when I no longer wanted him to catch me. Probably that was about the same time reliable "Daddy" became a stranger known as "Dad"—spoken often in impatience, occasionally with sarcasm, and sporadically with contempt. The many, many years when fear eclipsed the adoration, and the character flaws, to my way of thinking, far outweighed any redeeming qualities this appalling man ever could have possessed. How many years had I lost in trying to avoid, then deceive, and eventually just appease this man who had somehow become my adversary? How many opportunities had I squandered? How many dysfunctional relationships had I embarked upon? How many ailments had I provoked that were rooted in that mysteriously powerful father-daughter magnetism which, when displaced, repels rather than joins? So, for much of my life—actually for *most* of my life—I refused to let this man catch me.

But now the end is near. Not "the end" in that unconscious way that we all are vaguely aware of on a daily basis; nor even "the end" in that subconscious way that we come to terms with as we age and participate in the cycle of life; but rather "the end" in that harshly conscious way that follows the specialist's untreatable Stage IV prognosis.

And with the nearing of the end comes the awareness of that final opportunity to bring to my soul a modicum of closure and a measure of peace. A chance to acknowledge that stumbling and falling is not necessarily strange, deliberate, or unforgivable. To finally grasp the truth that that act of falling is an inevitable part of the human condition, but offering to catch the fallen—that is a highly desirable and wonderfully compassionate disposition.

And so today, after decades of misconstruing this man who I now realize is only human, I choose to embrace the humane. This day, as the springtime sun warms my face and my heart, I walk in a new state of readiness alongside this man who used to be my daddy, who morphed into my dad, and has finally evolved into my accepted and deeply loved father. I do this, not because he is perfect, but because, even though he fell—often, hard, and continually—I've finally learned what he spent a lifetime struggling to teach me—how to catch!

The Ring

Angelina Fast-Vlaar

"I have Joe's ring for you,"
the nurse whispers
as she passes me in the common room
of the Manor where Joe now lives.
"Come see me in the med room," she adds.
The empathy in her eyes does not
escape me, and I become aware
of the slight tremor in my hand
as I hold Joe's cup
while he sips his mid-morning coffee.

I leave him to munch on a windmill cookie
and walk to the small room adjacent to the nurses' station
where the medications are kept under lock and key.
The nurse reaches into a drawer
and hands me a small brown envelope.
"It keeps slipping off his finger," she explains.
I take the tiny package and
finger the circle of his love.
It's only a ring, I say to myself.
I feel a wave of emotion sweep over me.
It's only a ring…

I slipped it on his finger on that happy day,
nearly 20 years ago.
He looked so dapper in his dark tuxedo,
a striking contrast to his soft white hair.
His piercing blue eyes beckoned me, then
coaxed me up the aisle
until I stood beside him.
We promised to love each other 'till the end.
Take a deep breath—go outside.

I wheel Joe into the inner courtyard
where flowering shrubs, perennials, and annuals
create a tranquil atmosphere.
I place the wheelchair close to the fountain.
The sound of running water soothes.
It's only a ring...
Yet—it's another loss.
The journey with dementia is one
with many losses, and with each loss
grief rises to the surface.

I show Joe the ring.
"Remember we were married, Hon?"
"We were?" His eyes search mine.
"Yes, and I gave you this ring."
He touches it as it lies in my palm.
"And you gave me these."
I hold out my left hand and show him
the ruby encircled with diamonds and the gold band.
A faint smile creases his face.
I wrap my hands around his ringless fingers
and lightheartedly say,
"So why did you want to marry me, Joe?"
He is silent as he tries to process the question.
Then to my surprise he answers,
"Nice hair. Nice clothes."
I smile, but hunger for more.
"What else, Hon? What attracted you to me?"

For just a moment
the old familiar twinkle sparkles
as he repeats, "Nice hair. Nice clothes."
I squeeze his hands.
My eyes water.
The gift is so small, yet so precious.
And it's all he's able to give today.
I will gratefully tuck this gift away
with his ring.

The Right Thing to Do

Nonfiction

Ruth Smith Meyer

Turning from settling my tiny daughter in her carriage, I spun around to comfort our fifteen-month-old son, who had tripped over one of his toys. As I picked him up, I realized that the lunch dishes were stacked, still waiting to be done, and it was almost three o'clock. My heart sank. My days revolved around our two little ones and homemaking, however, it seemed I was always two steps behind in these duties that felt so mundane. Was it going to cause a major crisis if I didn't get the dishes done after each meal?

Up until my early twenties, I lived a rather sheltered life in a rural community and as part of a conservative, close-knit church. But, because of the extensive reading I'd been doing and a prayer group I'd joined, while I was pregnant with my second child, I began to struggle with the meaning and purpose of my existence. Most of the time I was happy with my life, but I longed to make a difference outside my little bubble. I desperately wanted to touch lives in the larger world.

As I thought about that, a brief doubt crossed my mind. If I was given an opportunity to do something outside of my usual boundaries, would my faith be strong enough? Would I even know what to do?

As I began washing the dishes, I asked God to provide opportunities to try my wings—but I have to confess I had no idea how anything could happen in what seemed like a constant circle of insignificant daily routine. It occurred to me that maybe I should be careful what I pray for in case I got an answer to my prayer before I was ready for it; however, I put that thought aside. I really did want a chance to do something that could make a difference for someone outside my small community.

The evening after my impulsive prayer, as we were finishing our meal, my husband asked, "Would you like to have a little outing?" He lifted our son from his high chair. "I need to return those tools to my dad, and I thought perhaps you and the children could ride along."

"Sure, that would be nice." Our new daughter was only a little over two weeks old, so I hadn't been out much recently. It was a lovely June evening, just right for a ten-mile drive through the country. "You won't be staying long, will you?"

"No, no! We don't even have to go into the house."

I quickly cleared the table and hurried to put a few things into the diaper bag. Then we were off.

When we arrived, we had a brief chat with Norman's parents, let our son play on the lawn with his uncle while Grandma held the baby, then started back home. It was nearing nine o'clock and we were within a few miles of our house when Norman pointed ahead. "What's going on up there?"

I looked up from tending our daughter, who was lying in my lap. No car seats or even seatbelts in those days.

A short distance ahead in the dusk, a little yellow Volkswagen, its passenger door open, was driving slowly beside a girl in a formal dress. She was walking in the grassy, uneven ditch. It seemed quite strange. As we neared, the door of the vehicle banged shut and the car sped off, spinning wheels and kicking up a cloud of dust as it disappeared over the edge of a hill ahead of us.

"Roll your window down and ask if she needs help," my usually cautious husband ordered as he slowed down.

As we pulled alongside, I noticed the sleeve of her dress was almost torn off and her skirt hung down, partly detached from her bodice. The young lady appeared to be in her late teens or early twenties. Her once-coiffed hair was now dishevelled. She was walking with one high-heeled shoe on. The other shoe, its heel broken, was in her hand. As her head turned at the sound of our approach, we could see her eyes large with fear.

"Can we help?" I asked.

"Can you give me a ride to somewhere safe?" she begged as she dabbed at her eyes with the back of her hand.

"Sure, hop in the back seat." With my free arm, I hugged our little son, who sat watching between me and his dad.

She wrenched the door open, jumped in, and slammed the door shut behind her. "Can you please go the other way? I don't want him to find me." The words, driven by fear, tumbled out.

Norman made a quick U-turn and headed back the way we'd come—the opposite direction from which the VW had disappeared.

"He tried to rape me," she sobbed. "I'm a mess. Thanks so much for stopping."

Norman looked in his rear-view mirror. "Oh-oh! He must have turned around. I think that's him coming up over the hill behind us."

Our guest threw herself down on the seat. "Please don't let him see me," she cried, her voice filled with panic. "I don't want you to get into trouble over me."

The little yellow vehicle sped past, but soon turned and came back toward us.

"He's turned back this way," Norman cautioned. "Stay down!"

Did he suspect that we had his prey? My heart pounded in my chest. I glanced at Norman and knew he was feeling the same way. But as the car drove by, we stared straight ahead pretending we had no interest in him.

At the first crossroad we came to, Norman turned left. Then he made a right at the next corner where a hill would soon get us out of sight of the main road. "I think we've lost him." He sighed in relief. "Now, where do you live, or do you want to go to the police station?"

"I want to go home," she sobbed as she sat up once more. "But I live in the city." When she named the street and the general area, we knew it was a good thirty-mile drive. "Maybe that's too far for you to go. I'd call my parents but I don't know if they're home yet."

"Don't worry! We'll take you to your home so you'll be safe." Norman glanced at me with a question in his eyes.

I nodded my approval.

As we entered a little town, Norman said, "We'd better stop for gas before we go any farther." When we turned into the service station, there was a loud clatter. "That sounds like the fan belt,"

Norman said, his voice betraying the exasperation he must have been feeling. "Guess we'd better fix that, too." He turned to look at our guest. "Are you okay?"

"Yes, I am now." Her voice caught on a left-over sob.

Norman got out of the car and talked to the attendant. While the young man began to fill the tank, Norman came back to the car door. "He says it may be twenty minutes or so before he can put the new belt on. Is that going to be a problem for you?"

"No, that's okay. Sorry to be so much trouble for you," our wounded little passenger lamented.

"No problem. Will the children be all right?" he asked me.

"They're happy right now and they will probably sleep once we're driving again. We can't go on with a broken fan belt, anyway."

As we waited, we noticed the little yellow VW speeding past on the road. Our guest quickly slunk down in her seat. "I hope he didn't see me!"

"I don't think he did," I said. "He was too intent on the road ahead." I turned to look at her, "Do you want to tell us what happened?"

She sat up again and sighed. "I'm Lori, by the way. I was a bridesmaid at my best friend's wedding today. He was one of the groomsmen. My parents were guests too, but they left before the dance started. They were going to their friend's house. I had to stay, because I was in the wedding party. My parents said they'd come back for me, but he—this groomsman—offered to take me home because he lives not too far from us. But when we left after the dance, instead of heading back to the city, he went in the opposite direction—away from my home and out into the country." She paused and I could hear tears in her voice again.

"Then he started coming on to me. I told him I wasn't interested and to please take me home, but he wouldn't listen. He stopped the car and started to—you know—I fought and kicked and screamed and scratched. He tore my dress and told me not to fight it. I managed to get the car door open and half jumped, half rolled into the ditch. My heel broke and my dress tore even more because he was hanging on to it." The tears started to fall again.

"I don't *ever* want to see him again!"

"I'm so sorry, Lori. Things like that shouldn't happen." What else could I say?

"The thing is—he's a friend of our family, and his wife is at home expecting their third baby at any moment. I had no idea he'd do anything like this or I'd never have accepted his offer to take me home." She blew her nose into the tissue I offered. "He said I must want it too, or I wouldn't have consented to ride home with him. I didn't even *think* of anything like that." Her voice rose and she emphasized each word of her next statement. "I did *not* want it, I *didn't*!"

"Of course you didn't! You mustn't blame yourself," I assured her.

We talked on until the minor repair was done. It took almost an hour.

As we drove toward her home, Lori grew silent and our children fell asleep. Now and then Lori roused to offer a little more information about her ordeal or ask about our family. Our children slept on.

When we turned into her street, she rejoiced to see her parents' car in the driveway and lights on. "I'm so glad they're at home. I would have been scared to go into an empty house. I would have been afraid he might be hiding somewhere. Mom and Dad are probably wondering by now where I am. I hope they believe my story."

"Do you want us to take you to the door and verify what happened?" my husband asked.

"No, no, I'll be all right. But thank you for offering. I don't know how it would have turned out if you hadn't stopped. It scares me to think about it. I don't know if I could have made it to the next house with only one shoe, and if I had made it to the house, he probably wouldn't have let me go in anyway. He was getting angrier by the minute. There was no way I wanted to get back in his car— that's for sure. I'm *so* thankful for what you did for me."

Lori got out of the car, but before she closed the door she said, "Thanks again!"

She walked to the house in her stocking feet, and turned at the door to wave.

We waited to make sure she got inside her home before we left.

  A Taste of Hot Apple Cider

On our way back, we talked about the whole episode and how our evening had turned out so different from what we had planned. Many questions arose in our minds. Had Lori's parents believed her? Were they supportive and comforting? If the man was a family friend, what would they do—confront him? End their relationship? Press charges? Would the wife find out? If she did, how would she feel, giving birth to a new baby while knowing the unfaithfulness of her husband? We still felt protective of Lori. How would she be able to avoid seeing her attacker again? How could she feel safe even in her own neighbourhood when he lived so close? We mulled over all these scenarios and more.

It was late when we got home. We carried our children in and tucked our son into bed, fed the baby, and then went to bed ourselves, but we couldn't settle our minds. We talked it all over again, and wondered what other things Lori might still have to face. Even after we finally went to sleep, my thoughts continued to swirl around and around.

It wasn't until the next morning as we shared our adventure with others that we realized the possibilities for personal danger that we could have faced. Our friends and family pointed out that sometimes an incident like that is a set-up by crooks to lure people in and rob them, or worse. They asked us what we'd have done if that irate, determined man had found out we had Lori? They all said we'd undoubtedly put ourselves and our children at risk in order to help her.

Those concerns hadn't even entered our minds, except maybe very briefly when we saw the man turning around and coming back our way.

Still, as we went over the night's happenings and examined the steps that we'd taken, Norman and I agreed that there was no alternative. Instinctively, we'd both known that the girl was in trouble. We'd sensed her desperation, and known we had to stop and offer assistance. Even when that little yellow car went speeding by us and then turned around and came toward us again, and it was obvious that he was trying to find out where Lori had gone, we'd only felt calm determination to keep her safe.

Maybe he was looking for her out of concern for her safety. We hoped that his better judgement would have returned. But we were quite sure he would have been experiencing some anger and probably fear of being found out. In any case, we still felt we had no choice but to help her.

On reflection, it occurred to us that our near-empty gas tank, the broken fan belt, and the delay in getting it fixed were God's way of making sure the coast was clear when we returned Lori to her home. We marvelled at how, when we did our part, God took care of the rest.

Was it only that afternoon that I had asked God to give me an opportunity to do something for someone else? What happened certainly wasn't what I'd expected could happen in my protected life, but God had answered my prayer. And the knowledge that I'd neither panicked nor ignored Lori in her need, but had actually risen to the occasion, gave me the courage I needed to be on the lookout for other opportunities—and they did come!

Although we never saw Lori again, we included her and her parents, as well as the troubled man and his wife, in our prayers for a long time after our encounter.

That experience increased our faith that God gives us grace and wisdom when times of crisis come across our path and it opened our hearts to other occasions to help. Whenever we thought of that night, we gave thanks that our first thought wasn't the possibility of danger or our own safety, but an instinctive desire to do the right thing in God's eyes.

  A Taste of Hot Apple Cider

Everybody Needs a Friend Who'll Tell It Like It Is

Nonfiction

Heidi McLaughlin

"Heidi," Maureen said, "I think you need to confront Aimee[1] and let her know how much she hurt you. If you don't deal with it, you risk the ugliness of internalizing your anger and nurturing a grudge."

I looked at my good friend, Maureen, who was sitting beside me on a bus en route from our home in Kelowna, British Columbia, to a Women's Conference in Calgary, Alberta. Was she joking?

Aimee, another friend of mine, had hurt me deeply by deceiving me and breaking a promise when I needed her the most. And now Maureen actually thought I should confront Aimee and tell her how much I'd been hurt by her actions? Like that was going to happen. Who was Maureen to tell me what I should do? Why should I listen to her?

Well, because nine years earlier, I had given her the right to tell me exactly what she thought.

As the Okanagan Valley burst into bloom in the spring of 2005, I'd approached Joanne and Maureen, two friends whom I'd first met as part of the leadership of a women's group in our local church. They were about my age, and they seemed eager to learn, had a similar sense of humour, and were willing to be vulnerable. I asked them a simple question: "Would you like to get together and start a book study this coming summer? I'm thinking that with our busy schedules, meeting every three weeks would work perfectly."

I was shocked yet delighted by their eager and immediate responses.

Right then and there, we decided we would meet at Joanne's home since it was the most accessible for all three of us. With contagious excitement we laid out the last details. We would meet at 6:30 and always start with a simple meal of soup, bread, cheese, fruit, and, of course, a delightful dessert. The very next day, I sent out e-mails organizing who would bring each food item, and who would lead the study the upcoming week.

We started with A.W. Tozer's book *The Pursuit of God*. With each chapter, we took turns assigning homework to help us understand the context of the Bible verses and the significance of each word, so that we could discover deeper insight into the meaning. Then, when we met, after sharing what we'd learned about the meaning of the verses, we'd set aside the books and papers spread across the dining room table and look into each other's eyes while we asked the hard questions, such as: "Do you ever get jealous? Do you struggle with insecurity? What are your biggest fears? Is pride a stumbling block?" With each question there would be long pauses followed by truthful and candid answers.

Joanne had created a beautiful home that shouts "welcome" as you walk through her doors. But as winter approached, I noticed that her hardwood floors were cold on my feet. One day while I was shopping, I spied some pink, orange and black striped fuzzy socks and I knew they would be the perfect item to warm our feet on those frosty winter evenings. When I presented my friends with these gifts, they smiled from ear to ear. Laughing the whole time, we pulled on our knee-high socks and started sliding up and down the hardwood floor. Over time, we began calling ourselves the "Sacred Sock Sisterhood."

The evenings we spent in our fuzzy socks continued to transform us as we became spiritually naked before each other, unashamed to share our dreams, fears, guilt and struggles. We discovered that when we became raw and honest, exposing the innermost parts of our souls to one another, and asked Jesus through simple prayers to help us remove our shame and guilt, we felt a soul connection that united our hearts like nothing else on this earth.

We believe this continues to happen as we allow the beauty and power of the Holy Spirit to work in our lives.

We became acutely aware that each person needs someone—a relative, colleague, church member, or friend—to walk with us, believe in us, listen to us, and accept us. We began to see that we are all created to do life with one another, and not live in isolation and fear.

In July of 2011, I was attending my daughter's fortieth birthday party, held in the backyard of one of her friends in southern Alberta. What fun to linger around a fire pit and interact with an eclectic group of my daughter's friends and neighbours—people from all walks of faith!

As I toasted marshmallows in the smouldering fire, I could hardly wait to squeeze a piece of milk chocolate between two graham wafers in order to create my all-time favourite classic—the famous s'more. But, gradually, my interest was caught by something else. Between dodging the smoke, licking sticky fingers, and laughing at corny jokes and zany birthday gifts, I realized I felt a sense of comfort and even belonging among this community of friends. As the sun went down and the campfire flames licked the dark prairie sky, I became engaged in an earnest and stimulating conversation with a young man who was passionate and honest about his relationship with God. Between bites of gooey s'mores, we asked ourselves this question: "With all the books, conferences, retreats, blogs and information about the love and power of God in our lives, why are so many relationships breaking down?"

We agreed that with the frenetic social media, and the disconnected lives we are pursuing these days, we often don't take the time to look into each other's eyes to unleash honesty and intimacy. We seem to be living segregated lives, pursuing our selfishly designed destinies without being accountable for any of our actions. But we're not created for isolation; we're created to live the life Jesus modelled for us through the "one another" principles. How do we achieve that kind of life in our busy world? Most important, how do we foster continued spiritual growth? My head bobbed up and down in resolute agreement as we both said the word, "Accountability."

Afterwards, as I thought back over the past years, I realized that applying the "one another" principles, accountability, and spiritual growth all happened in the Sacred Sock Sisterhood.

Over the years, Joanne, Maureen, and I shared our sins with each other and openly acknowledged our failures. Sometimes we've had to lovingly confront each other when we noticed jealousy or lack of commitment. All three of us have grieved the loss of our parents. Throughout these journeys of grief, our threesome validated our losses and prayed for each other. We've learned that we're all unique and that we need to accept each other exactly the way God has made us.

All three of us have enjoyed significant accomplishments as we stimulated and spurred each other on to write books, further our education, and take on influential and challenging leadership positions.

And that's why, as Maureen and I rode the bus to the conference, she called my attention to the fact that I was allowing an unresolved pain to foster a grudge in my heart, and that I needed to tell my friend Aimee that I was hurting about something we hadn't resolved.

Three weeks after the conference, Maureen again confronted me about the unsettled issue with my other friend. Lovingly, but bluntly, she asked: "Did you tell Aimee how hurt you were about what happened?"

I responded with a smile. "Yes, Maureen. I did. It was difficult at first, but we both decided that our friendship was worth the effort of being honest with one another."

I'll admit that it took me several days to process my feelings. But I knew that in order for me to have peace and restore our friendship, I needed to be genuinely forgiving.

I'm so glad I was held accountable by one of my Sacred Sock Sisterhood friends to deal with one of the most difficult but necessary "one another" commands that Jesus gave us: "Be kind and compassionate to one another, forgiving *each other* [my emphasis], just as in Christ God forgave you" (Ephesians 4:32).

Over the next few months, the pain from the fractured relationship slowly ebbed away, and I'm happy to say that we have remained friends to this day.

I'm so grateful that I have accountability partners who help me navigate through this messy and complicated life. I'm glad they remind me to forgive those who hurt me and not let jealousy, pride, or misunderstandings cause rifts in my relationships. None of us are smart or strong enough to succeed on our own.

Looking back, I realize that one of the smartest questions I ever asked was "Hey, would you like to get together and start a book study?" I had no idea I'd end up with two people who would courageously and lovingly walk through this life with me.

1. Name and situation have been changed to ensure anonymity.

Picture This!

Nonfiction

Kimberley Payne

I started taking pictures around my area in the fall of 2011 after my husband, Bob, surprised me with a Fuji digital camera for my birthday. For some time, I'd been taking thirty-minute walks around my village of Millbrook, Ontario. I did it for exercise, but I loved the beauty of the four seasons. I've always enjoyed being outdoors and seeing nature up close. I decided to take the camera with me on my walks in order to capture this beauty and take it home with me.

It became habit for me to grab my camera as I headed out the door for my walks, which quickly turned into moving photo-shoots. I took close-up pictures of leaves, grass, flowers, fences, mailboxes, trees, streams—anything that caught my attention. My favourite photos were close-ups of flowers. I entertained the idea of creating a blog to feature my pictures.

Over the next year, as the seasons changed, I found more and more opportunities for my photography. I took a picture of an abandoned birdhouse in the winter. It looked so lifeless and cold with a blanket of snow on its roof. A close-up of a dandelion in full bloom in the spring spoke to me that even in a despised weed there is beauty. A moss-covered bench in the summer reminded me of my need to not rush through life, but rather take breaks to enjoy the world around me. A wooden fence post in the fall captured my sympathy because it looked beaten and tired from years of service.

Every home in my country neighbourhood boasts at least an acre of land, so I found many interesting photo opportunities in the yards of my neighbours. One neighbour had grass that had grown three feet tall and sprouted yellow seeds. I captured the image before the seeds dropped. Even something as innocuous as grass can be beautiful when reflected in the right light and at the right angle.

One morning, the sun hit a large puddle on another neighbour's driveway in a way that clearly reflected a row of mature maple trees next to the drive. I quickly snapped it. Another neighbour had an old grey mailbox that leaned precariously to the left. There's just something romantic about an archaic mailbox. I wondered what letters had been delivered there over the years? What parcels?

With my digital camera, I had the luxury of taking picture after picture. Such a change from the old way where you had to pay for each photo you took! After every walk, I returned home and deleted shots that hadn't worked and transferred the rest from my camera onto my computer. Then I could see them on the full screen in all their intricate detail. I was delighted to see the quality and beauty of some of my photos. The digital camera had freed me to take pictures from angles and in positions that I wouldn't have tried before.

But as my "beautiful photos" file grew, I began to wonder what to do with them. It's one thing to take a pretty picture, but it adds so much more joy to share the photos with others who might also enjoy them. I asked some of my friends for ideas. Some said I should make the photos into greeting cards. Others recommended making them into a photo calendar. Still others suggested I put them on a board in Pinterest so anyone could see them. All good ideas, but none of them excited me.

Before bed one night, when I was praying, I asked God what He would like me to do with my pictures. Then I promptly fell asleep.

The next morning, I woke up with an idea running through my mind. What if I printed some of the best pictures, added a Bible verse to each photo, and hand-delivered them to my neighbours? That would not only give me a chance to use the pictures, but also help me meet my neighbours, and even allow me to share a little of my faith in a non-threatening way.

Since we'd moved to the area in 2002, I'd wanted to get to know my neighbours—partly to find friends in the area, and partly to share God's message of love with those who might not know Him. I'd prayed that I'd be able to do this, but somehow the time had flown and it hadn't happened. I knew that the biggest reason I hadn't done more to meet my neighbours was because I didn't know how to go about it or what to say to them. Now here was a way that might actually work!

I chose twelve pictures taken in the yards of twelve of my neighbours. Then I opened my Bible and chose twelve verses that either meant something to me, spoke of God's character, or were very uplifting. Three of the verses were favourites of mine: "Be still, and know that I am God" (Psalm 46:10); "Trust in the Lord with all your heart and lean not on your own understanding; in all your ways submit to Him, and He will make your paths straight" (Proverbs 3:5-6); and "I have come that they may have life, and have it to the full" (John 10:10).

Then I laboured to match each Scripture verse to the photo that best fit it.

I uploaded the photos to a free online website called PicMonkey, which let me edit each picture and type its Bible verse on it.

When they were all ready, I saved them and went to the website of the store where we get our photos printed to upload the pictures. I ordered one 6" x 4" print of each picture. The total cost was only $1.44! Plus they'd be ready for pick-up the very next day.

On my way to pick up the printed photos, I stopped at a dollar store to look for generic cards to slip my photos into. However, to my delight I found a do-it-yourself invitation kit that included everything I needed.

The kit cost only $2.00 and included a set of ten envelopes, ten 7" x 5" cardstock sheets, and a sheet of two-sided sticky dots. Although the kit was designed to send out wedding invitations, I planned to customize it to fit my needs. I bought two.

Once home, I peeled four sticky dots and placed them on the back corners of the 6" x 4" photo. Then I centred a photo over the 7" x 5" cardstock sheet so there was a one-inch border. On the back of the card, I wrote a simple note: "Dear Neighbour, I took this photo in front of your home. I hope you like it." I signed my name. Then I put the card into an envelope with the address of the house on it, and placed a return address label on the envelope. I did the same with the other eleven photos.

The morning I was ready to deliver the cards, I placed all twelve envelopes in a bag and set out on my walk.

As I approached the first home, however, I chickened out. I argued with God as I continued on my walk, hoping to gain courage. *Lord, what if they think I'm some religious nut? What if they think it's an invasion of privacy?*

Still worried about what my neighbours would think of me, however, I passed the next house without delivering the intended photo. But I'd been so certain God wanted me to do this!

I silently prayed for the strength to deliver the cards.

I realized that the next photo was the one of the leaning mailbox. I decided to put the envelope into the mailbox instead of going to the door. That was easy! I didn't have to talk to anyone or explain my actions. I just had to place the letter in the mailbox and flip the red flag to let them know they had mail.

I kept going, praying to God for help in getting over my fear of people. And praying that I'd be obedient to what I truly felt He was asking me to do.

With my heart in my throat, I walked up the long driveway of a neighbour I'd never met. Because of the sign with the picture of a German Shepherd dog on their front window warning strangers of a guard dog, and the loud barking I'd often heard from the back yard, I knew they had a German Shepherd. I wanted to leave the card in their mailbox, but there wasn't one! I considered opening the screen door and closing the door on the envelope, but I didn't want to bend or crease the photo.

Maybe if I knock, no one will answer. But as I got closer to the door, I could hear the sound of a television. My heart sank. *Someone's home.* Praying for courage, I took a deep breath and knocked on the door.

Moments later, the inner door opened and a woman about my age, with shoulder-length auburn hair, asked, "Can I help you?"

I stammered, "Hi, you don't know me but I live nearby. I like to walk and I like to take pictures." I handed her the envelope. "This is for you."

I was ready to turn to go, but she asked, "What is it?"

"I've always loved your fence and the maple trees behind it. It's a picture of them, reflected in the water on your driveway after it had rained. I hope you like it."

She opened the card and let out a small gasp. "This is my favourite scripture verse!" She gave me a big smile and explained that she was just working on a report for her church on how to reach out to people in the village. They were looking for new and creative ways to meet new people. "You're an answer to my prayer," she said.

I let out my breath and laughed. I explained my fear of approaching her home and the mission I was on delivering the photos. We talked about our churches and people we knew in common. She gave me her name and asked me to connect with her on Facebook.

"I can't tell you how relieved I am to have met you," I said. "I was so nervous coming here! Obviously God had this planned out." I showed her my bag with the rest of the cards. "I still need to deliver ten more photos. I'd really appreciate your prayers."

"You've got them!" She opened her arms wide to give me a warm hug.

As I walked down her long driveway afterwards, I couldn't help but laugh. What had started out as a simple hobby had ended as an answer to my prayer for God to use me in my neighbourhood to spread His message of love.

I looked up to the sky and whispered, "God, you truly are amazing. Thank you for giving me the courage to deliver that card. Thank you for orchestrating our meeting to inspire and encourage us both. You truly are a good and faithful Father."

After that, I had no trouble delivering the remaining cards, and I felt confident that God had a plan for each one of them.

Note: One of the photos Kim used had apple blossoms in it, so it was perfect to use here (see page 101).

My Love Affair with Gym

Nonfiction

Glynis Belec

Five years after I'd been diagnosed with ovarian cancer, I'd run out of excuses. It was time to stop blaming my illness for my weight gain.

Six months of chemotherapy along with heavy doses of steroids had sent my body into chaos. Sometimes I battled nausea, but more often than not the side effects of the steroids made me hungry.

For five years, I'd blamed the drugs for my weight gain, but I realized that people were starting to raise eyebrows whenever I whined about those awful steroids that made me blossom so.

I must confess, I kind of liked it when, at the beginning of my treatments, the oncologist said that it was good to have a bit of weight behind me during chemotherapy. I'm pretty sure he wasn't paying much attention to exactly how much weight I already had behind me!

During my treatments for ovarian cancer, the accompanying steroids kicked my metabolism into overdrive and food quickly became my BFF. Unfortunately, my doctor's words gave me an excuse to feed my ravenous appetite.

Soon, though, I noticed some of my clothes began to feel a little snug. I quickly relegated those to the "I can't throw them out because maybe one day they'll fit" section in my closet.

I steered clear of the bathroom scale lest it set my heart aflutter. I had enough to worry about. Weight gain was the least of my problems at that time.

When I thought about my added pounds, or mentioned them to others, I blamed my weight gain on anything my addled chemo brain could muster up at the moment—menopause, cancer treatment side effects, sore body parts, tiredness, and the list went on. But in my own mind, I blamed the steroids.

I more or less ignored my own responsibility when it came to the indulge/bulge cycle.

Then one day, reality slapped me in the face. While reading my Bible, I came to 1 Corinthians 6:19-20: "Or didn't you realize that your body is a sacred place, the place of the Holy Spirit? Don't you see that you can't live however you please, squandering what God paid such a high price for? The physical part of you is not some piece of property belonging to the spiritual part of you. God owns the whole works. So let people see God in and through your body."[1]

My stomach churned as I reread those words, and I knew God was trying to get my attention. I also realized that He'd been trying to get my attention for a while, but I'd been ignoring Him. Tears came as I realized that I had to stop justifying myself and start doing something about the excess padding that was clinging, uninvited, to my body. I knew God still loved me no matter how many bulges I had, but I also knew I had a responsibility to put on my big girl stretchy pants and start doing something about my weight.

The first step was to admit that my expanding girth and sky-rocketing poundage were no longer the fault of the steroids. Yes, the steroids might have been the beginning of the problem, but I had used them as an excuse for too long.

Step two was to do something radical—exercise!

After considering my options, I decided to sign on at the local gym. I was over-the-hill thrilled to learn that there was a twenty-four-hour access gym in our small town. Basically, the door is locked unless there is an attendant on duty, and every member has a pass key and can get in at any time day or night. You sign in and out using the key—computerized. I love it! Pretty fancy for a small town!

One of my biggest hesitations about "just doing it" was having to exercise in front of an audience. While I try not to care what others think about me, sometimes my vanity gets in the way. Too often, I end up comparing myself to some of the lithe, young bodies, barely into their child-bearing years. Wrong, I know. But it happens. Self-inflicted competition can be a cruel taskmaster. Vanity is worse.

Joe, the handsome young dude who runs the gym, helped me fill out the necessary paperwork, including a waiver in case of injury. He gave me copies of the paperwork, instructions on how everything worked, an access key, and a pep talk. Joe assured me that all was safe; the video cameras were always running, and I had free rein to come twenty-four hours a day, 365 days a year. Sounded good to me.

My original plan was to go to the gym in either the wee hours of the morning, in the evening if I could find a time when no one was there, or late at night if I could stay awake long enough. I didn't want anyone, especially young people, to see me jiggle and wobble like a bowlful of jelly. No one was going to laugh at me. (I'm sure they couldn't have cared less, but I wasn't going to take a chance.) Although I still wanted the facilities to myself, it was a little too challenging to keep myself motivated to get up early or stay up late. The easiest time for me to go was actually in the early evening. However, when I tried going at different evening times I discovered the place was filled with young buckaroos. So evenings were a bust.

After trying several morning and afternoon times, and always finding other people there, I discovered that midmorning was the best time for me because the other people who went at that time were mostly middle-aged grandmammas like me. Even though I didn't necessarily want to chat, that time slot worked well with my schedule and I didn't feel as if I stood out like a sore thumb among the other women who were my age.

I also discovered that going to the gym was a great way to catch up with local gossip—er, I mean news. So I stuck with the daily morning schedule.

Several weeks passed, and the scale began dipping in the right direction. I lost a few pounds and thanked God for nudging me into "reshaping" my temple. I didn't regret my decision to join the gym one iota. However, a part of me still wanted the facilities to myself. There were some exercises and a few pieces of equipment that I wouldn't dare tackle if anyone was watching, and I wanted to try them out.

I also thought it would be nice to be able to put on my praise music or switch to a different TV program, or just flip open a book and not be distracted as I performed my usual one-hour hamster routine on the treadmill.

One night—I think it was almost midnight—I couldn't sleep. It occurred to me that a trip to the gym was in order. I was also curious to find out if anyone else liked going at this time.

When I pulled into the parking lot, I was a little disappointed to see another vehicle, but I told myself to stop being so selfish. Maybe it was another middle-aged menopausal woman with bulges.

It wasn't. A well-built young fellow greeted me with a grunt as he bench-pressed what looked to me like a ton of weight. Luckily, he was just finishing up his routine—either that or I scared him away with my attempt at chatter. Whichever, within a few minutes, he packed up his kit and caboodle and nodded goodbye.

Grinning like a Cheshire cat, I flitted around the gym trying out pieces of equipment that I'd avoided for months. I even tried lifting a few of the big weights. But as I lay on a bench lifting a bar above my head, I envisioned it dropping and pinning me down and me being stuck with a 100 pound weight across my neck for hours and hours until some chuckling young buck came to my rescue. So I steered away from the heavy weight area and moved onto my familiar treadmill.

All went well for the first thirty minutes. Then I decided to increase the sound on the TV. I'm not sure if it was my heavy breathing or my grunting, but I had trouble hearing the program I was watching. I couldn't get the remote to work from my position on the machine, though, so I hopped off the still-moving treadmill and went closer to the TV. Presto, the remote responded and I was able to up the volume.

What transpired next is difficult to explain because it happened so quickly. I headed back to the treadmill and attempted to hop back on. Then my life flashed before me as I was catapulted backward. The remote control went up; I went down.

Thank goodness there was an interior wall directly behind me, separating the treadmill section from the exercise room; otherwise

Joe would have been wiping me off the wall at the far end of the gym the next morning. That said, I hit the inside wall with my back and fell to my knees in front of it as if I were praying. As if the hard landing wasn't enough, my knees ended up against the edge of the still-moving treadmill, where they burned like tires skidding on a road.

Oddly, I found myself laughing, even though I should have been crying (and praying). Within moments, I managed to untangle myself and get up to smack the "stop" button.

My knees were sore and raw, but like any good middle-aged wannabe athlete, I rubbed them for a few seconds, straightened out my stretchy pants, and got back on the horse. I did, however, cut short my workout by a few minutes.

Every time I look at the scars on my knees—yes I still have scars!—I'm reminded how blessed I am. Blessed that I didn't die that night. Blessed that I was able to get up, brush myself off, and keep going. Blessed that God loves me no matter how I look, and that he'll also nudge me to take care of myself.

I wonder if God might have had a bit of a chuckle that night, or if He winced as I hit that floor. I also wonder if I was thrust into that prayer position for a reason. I'm a visual, hands-on learner—the kind of person who requires a bit of a kick in the pants when it comes to keeping the focus.

All I know is that I'm glad I joined the gym. I'm still plodding along, doing my best. I feel fitter, stronger, and my clothes fit better. I'm also a whole lot safer since I've decided I'm better off sticking to the midmorning time.

One thing from that night still freaks me out, though—those video cameras are always running. If he wins, will Joe split the $10,000 prize from *Funniest Home Videos* with me?

1. *The Message*

My Journey to Joy

Nonfiction

Dorene Meyer

The foundation of my life is my relationship with God. Because of Jesus, I have hope not just for this life but for the next. There is also a sense of security; my life feels anchored even amidst the inevitable storms. I am so happy that I am a Christian, and I want others to experience what I have.

But there's one aspect of my life that I've always struggled with. Christians are expected to be joyful. I've heard it time after time in sermons where we're exhorted to be smiling and happy so that those who don't know God will see our joy and want to become Christians and can experience this wonderful feeling, too.

And I've come across it while reading my Bible. Verses like: "But the fruit of the Spirit is love, joy, peace, forbearance, kindness, goodness, faithfulness" (Galatians 5:22). "Be joyful in hope, patient in affliction, faithful in prayer" (Romans 12:12). And, "Consider it pure joy, my brothers and sisters, whenever you face trials of many kinds" (James 1:2).

Over the years, I have sincerely tried to be a joyful person. But, as with great sex, if you have to fake it, you don't got it!

It's not that I never feel joyful. My grandchildren are constant sources of joy to me. Every moment I spend with them is so precious. Recently, when I was saying goodbye to my youngest granddaughter, she blessed me with baby goodbyes (opening and closing her hands and bubbles of laughter). I love going on canoe rides and shopping adventures with my grandchildren, listening to their songs and stories, seeing their smiles, and feeling their hugs. I am truly blessed with a wonderful family.

As followers of Jesus, we're also part of a spiritual family. It says in the Bible (in John 1:12) that when we believe in Him, we become the children of God. Others who also believe in Jesus are our brothers and sisters. And there have been many times when I've felt that closeness and joy.

Yesterday, I went to church with my son and his family. Even though I didn't know anyone else, I immediately felt a oneness with the entire congregation as we joined together in worship to God. There was a time for spontaneous prayer, and from all over the room, one by one, people prayed out loud, asking God for something, thanking Him, or just telling him how wonderful He is.

In my heart, I was praying along with the speakers, and including my own prayers. And there was joy in those moments as I felt the Holy Spirit moving in the hearts around me. I've sensed the same encouragement and joy in my own community as well as in other communities of believers wherever I travel.

And yet, on my own, I struggle. I know intellectually that I have no reason not to feel that joy; but emotionally, I rarely feel it. I wonder if it's me; if something is missing in my life.

Recently, I began a dedicated pursuit of this elusive thing called joy.

In the classic C. S. Lewis book, *Surprised by Joy*, the author talks about the "deeply ingrained pessimism" of his youth, and explores some possible reasons for this. He cites three possible sources: early childhood trauma, the bombardment of pessimistic attitudes and words from his father, and frustration with his physical abilities. I looked at these areas in my own life and was immediately struck by the similarities.

I too, experienced childhood trauma. It came in the form of sexual abuse when I was very young, and I am so grateful that I am experiencing healing from it. I wrote about this journey in "Shards of Silence/Seasons of Hope" published in *Hot Apple Cider*. I have additionally written extensively on this topic in my novel series available from www.goldrockpress.com.

There is also within me a deep sadness and great empathy for all other children who have experienced or are now experiencing childhood sexual trauma. I feel constantly bombarded by the knowledge of the pain experienced by children around the world. We hear of so many who are being sold into the sex trade and I imagine their terror and pain. It doesn't seem right for me to feel joy when there is so much suffering in this world. I've learned in my studies that this hypersensitivity toward others is actually typical of abused children.

My sensitivity was heightened because of my upbringing. For the first four (almost five) years of my life, I lived in a First Nations community. During the remainder of my growing-up years, my mom was a foster parent to several hundred First Nations children. Because of this association, I've always been keenly aware of the trauma that many First Nations people suffered as children. Some as young as age four were forcefully removed from their parents to residential schools that were often hundreds of miles away. Some children didn't see their families again until they "graduated" at age sixteen. Some were more fortunate and were released in the summer. All were forced to speak a language foreign to them, and were from the first day of their incarceration forbidden to speak their own language.

There will always be a great sadness in my heart for all the children who suffered such awful loneliness, degradation, and deprivation. I know there is *nothing* I can ever do or say that will ever make up for what was done. Writing about it does at least help me to express what I feel. I was given an opportunity to do this with "Bannock and Sweet Tea" in *A Second Cup of Hot Apple Cider*.

The second thing C. S. Lewis spoke about was the bombardment of pessimistic attitudes and words from his father. Again, I can relate.

I am slowly disentangling myself from this same bombardment of pessimistic attitudes and words—but from my mother. It's truly frightening how long and deep the effect can be of words spoken to us in our childhood. I think we have come a long way as parents and teachers in thinking carefully about what we say to our children, but it is something we still need to be occasionally reminded about.

As for my father my feelings towards him are still conflicted. There was abuse in our lives before my mother left him, when I was four or five. No one talked about the abuse and so I grew up with vague but mostly positive feelings toward my absent father. I am still learning bits of information about my past, and I struggle to process the information as I receive it. In some ways, I would like the past, with all of its ugliness, to remain shrouded in darkness. But in my healing journey, I have learned that things brought to the light have a much better chance of healing. And although the act of peeling off the "onion skins" is incredibly painful, I know that the end result is a lifting of sadness and an increased measure of joy.

The third area Lewis mentioned, frustration with his physical abilities, might seem trivial compared to the first two, but I honestly believe this is an area that impacts many people, whether they realize it or not. I know it's affected my self-confidence and impacted my sense of joy, so these days, I'm intentionally working on it.

I've struggled with my weight since I was a child. I grew and developed early. I was the tallest person (even taller than the boys) in my class until I was ten, at which point I stopped growing in height but not in weight. I remember fasting for days and using those chewy chocolate squares (unbelievably called AIDS) for weight loss when I was in my pre- and early-teen years.

My highest weight was 225 pounds, and it's still a constant battle for me to keep my weight under 200. With extreme fasting, I can get down to 185, but that usually doesn't last long.

Over the years, I've come to recognize that two of the reasons for my being overweight have nothing to do with my metabolism. Both are related to the childhood trauma previously mentioned, and both are slowly losing their grip on my life.

One reason is a psychological impulse to pad my body as protection against predators. This is instinctive, not intentional. The goal is to look less appealing. Dressing in bulky clothes is also common. Over the past few years, I've worked hard to overcome this, realizing that I need to dress professionally and in an attractive manner in order to accomplish my goals as a college instructor and as an author. It's still hard for me to receive a compliment, though, especially from males. There is still an element of feeling unsafe if I look too attractive.

The other reason for my being overweight is an addictive behavior where food is similar to alcohol or drugs. Simply put, I feel happier and better able to cope with life after I eat. Food is something I can both enjoy and control, and I can choose to comfort myself with it.

But we all need food! So, now I'm struggling with taking the time and money to carefully make healthy food choices for myself.

While my children were young, I was very concerned about their nutrition, but over the past years, since my children have left the nest, I've found myself caring less about food preparation. Fortunately, my husband has stepped up to the plate, even finding that he enjoys cooking. But while he's at work (and I'm alone working from home), I too often find myself grabbing something quick to eat rather than taking the time to make something that is more nutritious.

Part of the reason stems from left-over feelings of low self-esteem developed during childhood. In a sense, I feel that if I'm just cooking for myself, I shouldn't "waste" time with food preparation. Recently, as part of my journey to joy, I have been purposely taking the time to do all the chopping and fussing with fruit and vegetables to make a healthy meal for myself.

But even then, I sometimes still find the old guilt hanging on, making me feel I've wasted time and money on myself instead of living a self-sacrificing life as I should. Even after making a meal that is nutritious and healthy for my body—a guilt-free meal—I still can't be truly thankful for what I'm eating.

Lately I've been following an online meal plan. Silly as it may seem, the affirmation I receive by following this plan (green means I did well that day) seems to help my attitude toward food.

Recently I've also joined a few friends who have formed an online support group dedicated to healthy eating and healthy living. It helps to know I'm not alone in this struggle. And, occasionally, I now find myself feeling some genuine gratitude toward the Creator for the food He's provided and for the active, healthy body He's blessed me with.

Three months ago, my sister told me that she has fourth-stage inoperable ovarian cancer. Since learning of her struggle, I've carried the ensuing sadness with me. Yet, as I write this article, I'm visiting with my youngest son and his family. I'm experiencing joy and laughter as I interact with my granddaughter. But at the same time, a part of me wonders if I have any right to joy when others are so sad.

I feel a similar sadness for people I don't even know. As a Christian, I understand that God loves us and created us for life, yet many of us turn our backs on our Creator and choose death. How can I feel joy when I know that so many people don't have this hope for eternal life?

Sometimes, I think maybe I'm one of those people who've been "blessed" with an overactive empathy gene. Maybe I was born with it. Maybe it came about because of my role as the older sister to hundreds of foster children. Maybe it's because of all the sermons I've heard about helping others, or all the Oxfam commercials showing starving children that I watched as a sensitive young girl. Whatever the reason, I seem to have developed this huge sense of responsibility for the entire world—past, present, and future.

Yes, you're right—it's a god complex! Daily, I need to remind myself that God is God, and I am not. Yes, He's given me a job to do on this earth, but He hasn't made me responsible for all of the jobs in all of the earth.

When I'm able to hold onto this truth, I find myself free to go about my day, doing the things I love to do, fueling my body with the nutritious food I need to do my job, and getting the rest I need to begin again the next day. And at those moments I feel joy.

I know I still have much to learn.

And so my journey to joy continues...

If you have any thoughts you'd like to share on this topic, please join me at http://journeytojoyjournal.wordpress.com.

Loving Play

Vilma Blenman

I watch them from our bedroom window
The duo in direct view
Enjoying loving play below;
He rolling his black and red police car
Down his driveway, then following it
Crawling on all fours, fast
So as not to miss the rear view
Of wheels twirling, a toddler's delight—
And oh the squeal on catching the car!
And now, car in hand, he rolls himself
To the edge of his driveway
While Mom watches, phone in ear,
A clear view from the open garage
And still he rolls on, farther away
Boy and pavement, a pair not parting
Boy in white T-shirt lying on black pavement
And I love the way she lets him
Love child's play.

I watch the way they play
And I love the way she lets him
Love and almost lose his car
In his game of chase and cheer;
Lets him lie in the grit and grime
Of damp dirt, without an angry word;
Lets him wander away and feel the
Danger of the sweet spot where sidewalk
Meets the road he knows he must not touch
And wonder whether she will know if he does…
"Hey, off the street, young man!"
I love the way he looks back at her
Hearing her, heeding her, smiling at her

Conceding yet all the time conspiring
Retreating to roll down his driveway yet again
An endless cycle of loving play
As if they have all day and more in store.

I watch true child's play
No matter it's now supper hour,
I watch through tears
And I don't wonder why
I want to take this gleaming glass jar
From the table by the window seat
And pour the settled sand
On our polished wooden floor
And sit with the scattered shells
Like a princess
On an enchanted island
In that play place
Swept clean so long ago.
But if the door should open
And someone should walk in—
Sand trailing, sand sticking to toes...
So I sit and watch the loving play below
And I marvel at the way
She lets him love his child's play.
It was never, I recall, *my* mother's way,
No, not at all our way to play.

Conversations in Baby Blue

Fiction

N. J. Lindquist

Sixteen-year-old Hailey Crawford opened her eyes to the sun shining brightly on a daffodil-yellow wall across from her bed. A baby was crying nearby. Presumably, that's what had awakened her. A tremor ran through her entire body as Hailey realized she was still in the birthing room at the hospital near her home, and the crying baby might be hers.

She lifted her head to look around. No baby here. Nobody here. She remembered a disapproving nurse saying she'd take the baby to the nursery, a groggy Ty saying he was going home to get some sleep.

Hailey sank back down on the pillow and shut her eyes. A kaleidoscope of fragmented memories formed in her mind. The suspicions, the tight feeling in her throat, the cold, clutching fear. Then the doctor's words—nine weeks pregnant.

The agony of telling Ty. His disbelieving, "Are you sure?" Shock finally giving way to accusation. In the end, weary submission. The impossible had happened. To them.

Her parents' stunned looks. Not their quiet, straight "A" daughter! Of course they'd never really cared for Ty, but they'd trusted Hailey. Hannah, maybe. Hailey's twin was much more inclined to rebellion and rashness.

Hailey remembered Hannah's incredulity. "But didn't you use a condom? Or the pill?"

All the tears and quarrels and making-up. The soul-searching. Abortion. Adoption. Running away. Marriage. Finally, the decision to keep the baby.

Poor Ty. At seventeen, he was nowhere near ready to step into the role of father. A couple of months ago, he'd told her he wished he'd never seen her. And yet he'd stood by. Gone with her to pre-natal classes. Coached her in the labour room. Given her a huge grin at the end. Awkwardly patted her hair and said, "You did it!"

Hailey was pulled out of her reverie by the opening of her door. A nurse about her mother's age came into the room with a cheerful, "Hi, Hailey, how are you feeling?"

Hailey forced a smile. "Okay, I guess."

The nurse grinned. "Something like a bowl of ice cream that's been left out in the sun?"

Hailey's smile grew. "Close."

"Well, don't worry. It won't last long. Dr. Patterson said you are just fine. He'll be by to see you later. And the baby is fine, too, but Dr. Patterson wants him to spend some time under a bili light. Just precautionary because you were RH negative and the baby was positive. I expect you know all about that?"

"They were supposed to give the baby an injection, too, right?"

"Yes, he got it, and all is well. I'll bring him to you so you can feed him in a little while. But what we need to do first is get you up and make sure everything is okay. If you want, you can have a shower, too. Or a bath." She turned to open the bathroom door.

Hailey stuck out her tongue at the nurse's back. The last thing she wanted to do was move.

"After you've gone to the bathroom, they'll bring you some breakfast. I expect you're starving."

Hailey was sitting cross-legged on the bed finishing her break-fast when the door opened again.

Ty walked in, wearing a sweatshirt and jeans, his hair needing a comb.

For a second, neither spoke. Then Hailey said "Hi."

"How ya doin'?"

"Pretty good, I guess."

"The doctor told me you did great. Five hours of labour is apparently short, especially for a first baby, and you had a pretty easy delivery."

"That's easy for him to say."

Ty grinned. "Where is he?"

"Still in the nursery. I just woke up not long ago. I was so tired. What time is it, anyway?"

"About nine-thirty."

"They said they'd bring him after I've had breakfast."

"He's a funny-looking little thing," Ty said. "You might send him back once you've had a good look."

"He's a baby."

"Yeah. A funny-looking one."

"Must take after you then!" She tossed a pillow at him and he ducked. "Why didn't you go to school this morning?" she asked.

"You're joking, right? I went home and got some sleep. In case you forgot, somebody woke me up at two a.m. to take her to the hospital."

"Yeah. Lousy timing, eh?"

"Yep."

"Why don't you sit down?"

He sat in the pale blue vinyl chair, ignoring the arm rests and leaning forward with his elbows on his knees. "You seen your mom and dad yet?"

"No." She held her breath. "You did call them, didn't you?"

"I sent them each a text."

She breathed again. "How did they respond?"

"They seemed excited. Your mom said she'd hoped it would be a boy."

Hailey smiled.

The same nurse as before came in just then. She was pushing a wheeled wood trolley with a baby lying quietly in the transparent bassinet on top.

Almost immediately, the baby began to cry, making a sound that to Hailey's ears sounded like "u-laaa, u-laaa, u-laaa." It made Hailey think of a lamb's "baaaa."

"Oh good," the nurse said. "You're both here. I just need a few minutes to go over some things to make sure you both know how to look after the baby."

Ty made a face. "Not me," he said. "Looking after babies is women's work." He kissed Hailey lightly on the cheek and left.

"You're sure you don't want to breastfeed?" the nurse asked Hailey.

She shook her head. "No way."

"You know breastfeeding is better for both of you?"

"Yes, I've heard it all, but I don't care. I'm going back to school so my mom will be looking after him. Besides, I don't want to. Plus my mom didn't, either, and we're okay."

The nurse got out a bottle that held formula and gave it to Hailey. Then she positioned the baby in Hailey's arms. "Be careful. You have to hold his head."

"I know. Ty and I went to the classes."

"Oh, of course." The nurse looked down. "I'm sorry, but you seem so young."

Hailey picked up the bottle and aimed it at the baby's mouth. "Is this right?"

Feeding the baby turned out to be very easy. He was obviously hungry, and he instinctively seemed to know what to do to get the milk.

After a few minutes, the nurse left them alone.

When the bottle was empty, and the baby asleep in her arms, Hailey sat back and smiled. This mothering thing was easy.

After a little while, the nurse returned to take the baby back to the nursery and the bili light. "Now there's a contented baby," she said. "Good job."

Soon after, Hailey fell asleep.

Hailey woke to the sound of familiar footsteps in the hallway. Her heartbeat quickened as a petite blonde woman and a comfortably stout man entered the room. They both carried floral arrangements.

As the woman kissed Hailey on the cheek, she exclaimed, "I was just telling your dad I can't believe how little time elapsed between when you called Ty to come get you and his text to say the baby was born! When I think of the hours of agony I had to endure waiting for you and Hannah to come— Why, you barely know what labour is!" She looked around. "What a nice room. They didn't make them like this in my day! These flowers are from us. Don't you just love this little puppy vase? And the matching balloon? Where shall I put them?"

Hailey waved in the direction of the windowsill. Her mother moved toward it, and her father came forward, carrying two more bouquets. He leaned forward to kiss her cheek and then held out the flowers.

"The ones in the bootie thing are from your Aunt Katy and Uncle Jim, and the ones in the lamb are from Grandma Crawford."

"They're lovely," Hailey said. "Can you thank them for me?"

After arranging the flowers on the windowsill, Hailey's mother said, "Can we see the baby? Will they bring him here or what?"

"I don't know. He was here not long ago. Maybe you can go to the nursery and ask to see him."

When they were gone, Hailey lay still, thinking of all the turmoil caused by this tiny being who belonged to her. Her son. What a funny word. Hailey and Ty's son.

Her parents returned twenty minutes later.

"He looks just like you," her dad said with a smile.

"He's so tiny," her mother said. She frowned. "So fragile. And you're so young to be responsible for a newborn baby."

It was true, of course. And at thirty-five, her mother was far too young to be a grandmother.

"Ty said he'd pick up the car seat and the other things after school today."

"All right. But I may not be there. I have some shopping to do. I had to wait until I knew if it was a boy or a girl."

Hailey heard the accusation behind the words. Her mother had wanted to know the baby's sex ahead of time, but Hailey and Ty had decided not to find out. They liked the idea of a surprise. That was another area of contention.

Hailey said, "Ty knows where the spare key is."

"Yes, he does." Another world of meaning was behind those words, too, but Hailey chose to ignore it. Everything had already been said too many times.

Her dad cleared his throat. "Does he have a name yet?"

Hailey shook her head. "We wanted to wait until he was here."

Her mother said, "You'll need to pick one. You need to register it as soon as possible."

"I know. Ty and I will talk about it later today."

"Robert would be nice," her mother said. "After your grand-dad. Or Christopher."

"We have a list, Mom."

Fortunately, Dr. Patterson came into the room. He told them everything had gone well. Hailey had had an easy birth, the baby was very healthy, and he'd confirm in the morning, but he thought they'd both be able to leave the hospital by noon the next day.

Shortly after the doctor left, her parents left. Her dad had to get back to his office and her mom had an appointment at the hair salon.

Hailey fell asleep.

She woke up when Ty came in. "It must be nice to be some people," he teased.

"Some people just had a baby."

"If they did, they must have been crazy."

Ty leaned over and kissed her. Then he set a backpack on the end of the bed and sat in the armchair. "You've sure got a big-mouth for a sister."

Hailey sat up. "Why?"

"I decided to go to second class. So then I found out that your big-mouth sister had already told everybody about the baby. I figure it's my kid, I should be the one who tells everybody. But not with her around."

"I guess she didn't think."

"I bet she did it on purpose. I told you she doesn't like me."

"You don't like her either."

He shrugged. "Don't say anything to her. Don't give her the satisfaction of knowing she bugged me."

"Okay."

There was silence for a few minutes.

Ty undid his jacket. "So, old man Watson congratulated me. What a laugh! Me and the guys were talking about the baby, right? So Ron asks Watson if he's heard that Hailey had a baby. So then everybody's staring at Watson, and he had to say something, so he says, 'Congratulations, Tyler,' and you could tell it killed him to say it. What a laugh!"

Hailey didn't say anything for a moment. Then she asked quietly, "Does the whole school know?"

"I guess. You can't keep something like that a secret. When you changed schools most kids figured something was up."

"Yeah, I guess so." She sighed.

Hailey's lunch tray was brought in.

"Do you have homework?" she asked Ty when they were alone

"Watson gave us a whole bunch of junk. Likely on purpose because he knew I wouldn't do it."

"You will so do it."

"The heck I will! It isn't every day my girl has a kid. He should be good for at least one free day."

"I'll help you with it."

"Here?"

"Why not?"

While Hailey ate lunch, they worked on Ty's homework. "Don't you need to get back to school?" she asked finally.

"Yeah, I guess. See you later." He snatched the cookies from her tray. Then he put them back. "I guess I should be nice to you for a while, huh?" He left.

The next few hours passed quickly. She fed the baby again and then fell asleep. She didn't wake up until Hannah and two of Hailey and Hannah's friends came in.

Hannah plopped down on the bed. "So where's the kid?"

"Ow!" Hailey yelled.

Hannah jumped up. "What's wrong?"

"If you have to sit there, at least do it more gently and don't sit on me."

"Oh, sorry. I'll be more careful."

The three girls stayed for over an hour.

Long before they left, Hailey felt like screaming at them to leave her in peace. They talked mostly about school and about how silly Ty had looked bragging about how he'd gotten his girl in trouble and now had a baby to look after, and how many students and teachers had asked Hannah how "poor Hailey" was doing.

They had to see the baby, so Hailey sent them to the nursery to see if he could come down, and when they returned with him in his bassinet, wished she hadn't. They didn't seem to know the first thing about how to hold a small baby, and she was terrified they were going to drop him.

By the time they left, Hailey had a headache. She sat there holding her child, studying his tiny face. It seemed to her his head was shaped the same as Ty's, but his nose and mouth were hers. His eyes were blue, but she knew they might darken.

How amazing that this tiny life belonged to her! And how frightening. What was it the Children's Aid lady had said when she'd paid Hailey a visit a few weeks ago? She'd encouraged her to give the baby up for adoption. She said that tests showed that children of teen mothers are more likely to experience child abuse and neglect than children of older mothers. But Hailey couldn't understand that. She'd look after her baby. She'd never hurt him. How could anyone hurt something as sweet as this?

Hailey got up to put him back in the bassinet and caught a glimpse of the two of them in a small mirror someone had hung on the wall on the side. As she stepped closer to the mirror, she had a flashback to a picture she'd seen a million times on the walls of the Catholic schools she'd attended. It was one of the Madonna and Child. Mary was holding the baby, who wasn't much bigger than hers, with her cheek resting on the top of his head. They both had their eyes shut. Mary must have been about her age when she had her baby. And now Hailey had a baby. This was her baby. Her son. "Hailey's having a baby" wasn't a concept anymore. It was real. She was a mother. Hailey shivered.

Instead of placing the baby in the bassinet, she sat down on the blue chair and cradled him against her so she could gaze into his face while tears filled her eyes and splashed on his blanket.

She was still sitting in the chair when Ty came in. "Oh, they let you have him, huh?"

"Do you want to hold him?" she asked. "You can if you want."

"Me hold him? You gotta be kidding." He sat down. "You look like you're doing just fine."

"Chicken."

"Put the kid down and say that."

Hailey smiled. "Look how tiny he is? Can you believe you were once that small?"

"I wasn't. This little runt is only seven pounds. My mom says I was nine. Speaking of my mom, has she been here?"

"No. Is she coming?"

"If she doesn't, I may never speak to her again."

Ty's parents had both been opposed to Hailey's keeping the baby. Only with great reluctance had they agreed that Ty and Hailey could get married at the end of the school year. "Don't worry about it," Hailey said. "If they miss seeing their newborn grandchild, it'll be their loss."

There was a knock at the door and Hailey's mother came in carrying several packages. "Oh, hello, Ty. How do you like him?"

"He won't hold him," Hailey said.

"Well, I will if you'll let me." She set the packages on the bed.

Hailey looked at Ty. "Do you want to hold him for a minute first, Ty? I'll help you."

"Come on, Ty!" her mother said. "You have to learn some time."

"Oh, all right." Ty hesitantly took the baby from Hailey. After holding him stiffly for a few minutes, he said it was her mom's turn. A few minutes later, he left.

"I hope Ty didn't leave because I came."

"No," Hailey lied, "he had homework to do."

"Speaking of that, do you still think you'll be ready to go back to school next week?"

"Sure. Why not?"

"It's going to be funny having a baby around the house again."

Her mom seemed at ease holding the sleeping baby.

"Oh, and be sure to tell Ty he can come over whenever he wants. And help bathe him or whatever. After all, it's his baby too."

Once more, Hailey held her tongue.

Still holding the baby, her mother picked up a shopping bag and handed it to Hailey, who opened it and pulled out a small blue knit sleeper with a matching cap.

"How do you like it?" her mother asked. "I thought he could go home in it."

The two of them spent several minutes admiring the clothes and other items her mother had bought. Then her mother put the baby into the bassinet. There were a few more things she wanted to buy before the baby came home the next morning. "Sleep well. Your dad has work to do tonight, so he won't see you until tomorrow." She paused in the doorway. "Don't forget you need a name."

"Yes, Mom. I know."

Hailey's mother had been gone only a few minutes before Ty came back into the room.

Hailey looked up. "Mom said she hoped you hadn't gone because she came."

Ty laughed. "I bet. She saw me in the hall and had the nerve to tell me I can come to your house to see the baby any time I want. As if I need her permission to see my own kid! Maybe I'll never come over. That'd show her."

In a soft voice, Hailey said, "It would show me, too."

"You've got nothing to complain about. I'm going to marry you, ain't I?"

"Aren't."

"What?"

"You said 'ain't.'"

"Sorry. I'm not the English genius. That's you."

"It doesn't matter."

The baby began to fuss. Not quite crying, but making what Hailey took to be unhappy sounds. She got up and picked him up. "You're getting hungry, aren't you?"

"What?"

"The baby." She rocked him. "If you're hungry all the time, you'll soon be as big as your daddy."

"More like as fat as your grandpa."

"My dad isn't fat."

"Oh, sure. And I suppose you want me to believe he and your mom get along, too."

She changed the subject. "What are we going to name him?"

"I don't know. Just so long as you don't get any crazy idea about naming him after your dad or anything."

"We could name him after you."

"Thanks, but no thanks."

"Okay, how about Austin? That's the name that popped into my mind this morning when I saw him first."

"If you want."

"Do you like it?"

"Yeah, sure."

"I'll see what my parents think."

"Why? It's your kid. Name it what you want. If you like Austin, then that's what it is. Okay?"

"I guess."

"How long do you have to stay here?"

"Just until tomorrow."

"Good. It's depressing here. The smell bugs me." He stood up. "Ed's getting some beer, so me and some of the guys are going to celebrate tonight."

"Ty, you shouldn't."

"You worry too much. See you tomorrow."

"Don't forget you have to pick up the car seat from my house. And you're going to come to get us at noon, right? Come straight over after class?"

"Yeah, sure." He stepped toward her and kissed her hungrily.

The baby began to cry.

Hailey pushed Ty away so she could rock her baby.

Ty frowned. "Is he going to cry all the time?"

"He's hungry. Can you tell the nurse I need a bottle?"

Ty left.

A few minutes later someone brought a supper try for Hailey. Moments after, a nurse brought a bottle for Austin.

Hailey decided to eat first, then feed Austin, but she'd only taken a few bites before he began to cry in earnest. She picked up the bottle. Afterwards, she ate her cold supper and sat for some time thinking about the future.

She was startled when her dad walked in. "I didn't expect to find you alone," he commented as he gave her a quick kiss on the cheek, set a box of chocolates on the night table, and sat in the chair. "Feeling okay?"

"Pretty good. Probably the younger you are, the easier it is."

"Yeah. You know, your mom wasn't much older when you and Hannah were born."

"Is that why you got married?"

He looked disconcerted. "Well, er, your mom was nineteen and I was twenty-one. That's a lot different than you and Ty." He stood up. "Well, I've got a lot of work in my briefcase, so I guess I'd better go. Just wanted to bring you some chocolates. Bye, Sweetie-pie."

After a few minutes, a nurse came in to take the baby back to the nursery and Hailey fell asleep.

She was lying there awake when Hannah came in.

"How's it going?" her twin said.

Hailey's defenses immediately went up. "Fine."

"Really?"

"Yes, everything's fine."

"Right. You have a new baby, a boyfriend who's a jerk, and parents who think fighting all the time is what normal people do, and everything's fine."

"Don't forget the sister who's always putting me down."

"Oh, yeah, I'm your biggest problem."

"Ty isn't a jerk. Not compared to the guys you date, anyway."

"But I use protection. And if an accident should happen, I'd get an abortion in a heartbeat."

"Well, that's you. Not me."

"Duh."

"So why did you come? To gloat?"

Hannah stood up and walked over to the window. She picked up one of the floral arrangements and studied it. Then she picked up the next one. As she set it down, she turned. "I don't know why I came. I guess it was to tell you to think carefully about what you're going to do. I know you think you want to keep the baby, but maybe you should think about the baby and what he needs."

"Austin."

"What?"

"His name is Austin."

"Okay, Austin. Think about what's best for him."

"You won't understand, but I already love him. He's so cute and helpless. And he needs me."

"He's not a puppy."

"I know that."

"Mom and Dad never let us have a pet."

"I know."

"Well, think about what's best for Austin, not for you. Forget about the novelty of having a baby, and think about what it will be like for him to have teenage parents, and Mom and Dad and Ty's parents as grandparents. Just think good and hard about it. That's all I came for." Hannah left the room.

Hailey turned her face to the pillow and began to cry.

Sometime later, a nurse brought Austin so she could feed him. All went well, but the second time, in the middle of the night, he started spitting up and crying after he'd only taken part of the bottle.

Frustrated, Hailey carried him to the nurse's station, where a dour older nurse showed her how to burp him and answered a few other questions. After that, he was okay again. But it was a long time before Hailey went back to sleep.

  A Taste of Hot Apple Cider

She'd just finished breakfast when her mom came in. "Have you picked a name yet?"

"We've decided on Austin."

"Austin? But, don't you think—?"

"Ty and I like Austin."

"Well, I guess Austin's okay. It could be a lot worse."

"And we'll register him under Ty's name."

"I'd have your father check that. There might be some legal implications. Don't do it yet." She stood up. "I'm going to run out and get a few groceries now so I can be there when you get home." She started toward the door and then turned back. "By the way, Tyler hasn't picked up the car seat yet. Are you sure you still want him to bring you home?"

An hour after her mother left, Ty appeared.

"Shouldn't you be at school?" she asked. "I thought you were coming to get me at noon."

"I skipped. Stupid teachers drive me crazy. Nothing ever makes them happy."

She didn't comment.

He picked up one of the items her mother had brought. "What's this stuff?"

"Mom bought clothes for taking Austin home."

He paced around the room, "She's so bossy! You know what's going to happen, don't you? He's going to be her kid, not yours. She's going to be home with him all day, and when you get home, she'll say, 'Don't bother him. He just went to sleep,' and she'll tell you when you can pick him up, and if we want to take him out with us she'll have some reason why we can't. It'll be like he's her kid."

He spun around and glared at her. "I've had it to here with all of them! My folks only asked once how you were and that's it! And your stupid sister makes me sick! Her and her snooty friends. She couldn't care less how I feel. Man, I wish somebody'd get her pregnant! Then she wouldn't act so high and mighty. And your so-called-friends. 'How's Hailey?' in those syrupy little voices. I felt like throwing up. I don't think anybody cares how I feel!"

"I do," Hailey said quietly.

He took three quick steps and sat beside her on the bed. She held him as he kissed her. After a while, she said, "We'll get through the next few months somehow, and then we'll be married and everything will be okay."

He drew back. "Oh, sure. All I have to do then is work and go to night school at the same time. If I can get a job. And you'll have to work, too. And we'll have to drag the kid everywhere we go."

Hailey straightened up. "It wasn't my idea to get pregnant."

"Well, it sure wasn't mine."

Tears started and she looked down.

Ty raised her chin. "All right, let's not start on that again." He got up and walked over to the window. "I guess it's just that now that the kid's really here, it all seems more… I don't know… Real, I guess. Like there's no escape."

"You don't have to marry me."

"It ain't—isn't—that. It's just… Oh, forget it, okay?" He came over and kissed her again, holding her so tightly it hurt.

A little while after Ty left, a nurse brought Austin. Hailey held his tiny body close. He was so warm and cozy. And so helpless. She thought again of the picture of the Madonna with her Child.

If anyone asked her parents what religion they were, they'd say Catholic, and they'd sent their daughters to Catholic schools, but they only went to Mass roughly twice a year, at Easter and Christmas. Otherwise, God had no place in their lives.

But when Hailey was ten, she'd talked her parents into letting her go to a different church's camp for two weeks one summer. Her best friend at that time was going, and her friend's parents were going to be on staff, so Hailey's parents finally agreed. At the camp, Hailey had learned the story of Mary and her baby—how God sent His son to be born in a stable, and how He died and came to life again.

Now, she wondered how Mary felt as she held her tiny son that first night. Had she worried about the future? Or had she trusted God to look after her son?

As Hailey held Austin and gently patted his back the way the nurse had shown her, tears filled her eyes. What did the future hold for the little life she had brought into the world? And why, with so many people around her, did she feel so alone?

"Oh God," she whispered, "I don't know if you're real or not." Tears dropped onto Austin's blanket. "God, if you're really there, would you help me, please? And help Austin. He's so small, and I want him to know what it means to be loved, and to be safe."

A verse came into her mind. She'd won a prize for learning it at the church camp. She even remembered the reference: John 3:16. "For God so loved the world that He gave His one and only Son, that whoever believes in Him shall not perish but have eternal life."

On the second to last night of the camp, she'd asked God to forgive her from her sins, and prayed that Jesus would come into her heart. But when she got home and told her parents what she'd done, they'd laughed. Hannah had told her that only stupid people believe in God. So she'd locked that moment away. Until now.

What if her parents and Hannah were wrong, and God was real after all? Hailey looked pensively at her son's sleeping face. Then she took a deep breath. In her heart, she knew what she had to do. Maybe Hannah had been wrong before, but this time she was right.

"It'll be okay, Austin," she said. "I'll take good care of you. Promise. Tomorrow, I'll talk to the Children's Aid lady and ask her to make sure she finds a really good family to adopt you."

Tears filled her eyes. "I'm going to miss you so much, but I know it's the right thing to do. And who knows? Maybe God will even help me see you again someday. Until then, I'll pray for you every single day, Austin. That's the best thing I can do for you now."

Note: This story is fiction, but it's based on a true story. N. J. once shared a semi-private room in a maternity ward with a teen mother. Unable to avoid hearing a lot of what was said on the other side of the flimsy cloth curtain, N. J. ended up making notes and later wrote the first draft of this story. Ironically, years later, N. J., who was adopted, learned that her birth mother wasn't quite 16 when she was born. N. J. is currently writing a memoir titled *LoveChild: Reflections From a Former Ugly Duckling*.

From Hard Places

Nonfiction

Carmen Wittmeier

She looks more like a doll than a baby, I thought when they brought her to our front door. I knew the difference: I was ten years old and pretty much a pro when it came to being a foster sister.

"This is Samara.[1] She's four months old," the social worker said to me and my seven-year-old brother in the high, silly voice some adults use with kids. She flashed my mother that look—the one that told me I had better pay attention. This adult was hiding something.

My mother had told us that we were getting another foster baby, but this baby was a big disappointment. She was pale and pasty, and when you looked at her, she didn't even look back. When you smiled at her, her mouth didn't move. She wasn't a real baby, a human baby, a fun baby; she was what the social worker called "a failure to thrive." Everything about her was wrong.

My mother sat me, my younger brother, and my older brother down on our rickety beige couch and tried to explain how Samara's mother, loving her baby but lost in the maze of mental illness, had difficulty finding Samara. Sometimes, my mother said, she didn't even remember that she had a baby, and so Samara had spent her life confined to a crib in a small apartment, her cries for food and love mostly unanswered. Presumably there was a father, but he wasn't around. As her mother struggled to simply exist, Samara stopped trying altogether. She no longer even bothered to cry, and how, without exercise, her body had grown fleshy and limp.

But over the next few months in our house, our lively house with three children and an assortment of pets and messes and squabbles and hugs and friends tramping in and out, this baby returned to life. Her eyes began to focus and she started to track the voices and objects around her. As her face brightened, a crooked smile came out of hiding. Then she learned to laugh and to crawl like a hellion, to eventually speak and, thanks to our tutelage, to bark like a dog. She sprouted hair—pale locks that barely covered her crumpled ears. She became, to my ten-year-old eyes, human in every way.

As Samara grew, so did her obsession with kitchen cupboards and the treasures they held. When certain that she was alone, Samara would reach out to rest her chunky hand on the wood that separated her from the pots and the pans. Then, remembering the last "No!" she would withdraw. Moments later, the concealed prizes would inevitably beckon her, call her by name, overwhelm her toddler brain. And my little brother and I would wait, concealed, like cats waiting for that perfect moment to pounce.

The hand would reach; the drawer would open. "No!" my little brother and I would shout victoriously, and Samara would jump and wail. And then, our mischief completed for the day, we would console our little foster sister. We would hold her, and tickle her, and toss her in the air, and chase her across the floor until she crumpled into a ball of laughter. My older brother, more dignified, would simply pick her up when he came home from high school, set her on his chest, and nap on the chesterfield with her happily nestled against him.

Then, one day, Samara's troubled mom took her own life, changing the landscape of our lives. Samara had celebrated her first birthday only two months before the social worker returned to carry her out through our front door—the same door used when each of our fourteen foster babies was taken from us. We were told that Samara was going to a new home, to be mothered by a disabled woman who understood that beautiful things grow from hard places.

I was twenty-four when I first saw Elisha, a little girl with hair the colour of flames. There she was, pressed against the window next to her front door, the pane of glass smeared with fingerprints. I learned later that she'd been waiting there for me for two solid hours.

She quickly looked me over, and found me wanting. "I was hoping they'd match me up with a blonde Big Sister," she said. But since I was the only option, she decided to keep me anyway.

I had no issue with my brown hair, and I thought myself worth keeping. I was young and reckless enough to believe that one person could change a life, dismantle the system, transform the world. I had weathered the chaos of all those drooling and dribbling foster siblings, and had witnessed love's transformative power firsthand. Nevertheless, I had no idea what I was in for as Elisha's Big Sister. Nothing in my life—not even the antics of one particular foster sister known for dancing on table tops, pulling down bird cages, and tumbling down stairs—had prepared me for the dramatics of a teenager trapped in a first grader's body.

That night, I was scolded for assuming that a pet store was an appropriate destination for our first outing. "We need to spend money," my Little Sister insisted. "That didn't cost anything. What were you thinking?" She rolled her eyes with a sophistication that made me forget she was only six.

And thus it began: the push and pull of our relationship, me wanting to model my solid Christian values, my Little Sister intent on purchasing every knick-knack and plastic amusement conceivable. She was convinced that I'd leave her in a matter of weeks, and she wanted something to show for it, even if it ended up in the trash.

I learned, fairly quickly, that the traditional values that had served me well didn't apply to her world. In her experience, boldness, cunning, and knowing how to work each situation to gain the advantage were all that mattered.

And this little girl, whose mother had left, divorcing her father when Elisha was only three, was resourceful.

One evening, after chatting with Elisha's dad in the kitchen, I joined Elisha in her bedroom. She was sitting on her bed, scissors and a pair of jeans in hand, labouring in earnest.

I sat on the bed beside her.

"I'm making a new wardrobe for summer," she said conversationally as the bottom half of a denim leg fell to the carpet.

I frowned. "Did you ask your dad if you could do that?" It looked to me that my Little Sister had transformed—or rather hacked—a pair of her jeans into shorts. They weren't shorts of a functional variety; they weren't even the short shorts that a teenager might wear to compliment her dark streaks of eyeliner and exposed midriff. These were the shorts so short that they could secure a place in the *Guinness Book of World Records*.

As it turned out, Elisha's father didn't approve. And ten minutes later we were back in her room, my Little Sister thoroughly chastened.

Wanting to be helpful, I pointed out that this sort of catastrophic event typically blew over in a few days, that she'd made an honest mistake, and that she might still someday make a name for herself in the fashion industry.

"You don't get it!" She pouted. "I didn't just cut *one* pair of jeans for summer. I made *all* my jeans into shorts. And I made *all* my skirts into miniskirts, too. I told you I was making a wardrobe."

She stood there mournfully, a small girl fully aware that her childhood might very well be at an end. She wasn't emotional, since she believed her actions were perfectly justified; she simply wanted to figure out how to avoid punishment. We grappled with the ethics of our now mutual predicament.

"You've got to tell your dad everything," I said.

"I'll put them in the dumpster in the back alley. My dad will never find out."

"But then what will you wear?"

She hadn't thought of that.

"Tell the truth," I urged. "It's the right thing to do. It's the only thing to do."

After a few minutes of agonized strategizing, she finally agreed on a compromise.

"You go downstairs and tell the truth," Elisha said. "I'll be up here in my room crying."

This incident would blow over in a short time, as would Elisha's idea to bury her twelve-year-old brother's most precious keepsakes in the flower garden where neither moth nor rust could corrupt. Over time, her struggle to preserve the remnants of a brief childhood would only intensify. At age seven, she moved into her mother's apartment, where she was expected to fend for herself and to steer clear of the illicit adult activities taking place around her. Elisha's refrigerator was almost bare: dinner consisted of a lonely walk to a nearby convenience store to purchase one plastic-wrapped sandwich, a bag of chips, and a bottle of pop.

Through it all, Elisha's imagination remained startling, and vivid. She believed with conviction that applicants applied annu-ally for the position of the Devil and that her new stepmother was a shoe-in. Nothing could sway her from her belief that the Tooth Fairy was a six-foot-tall bicuspid, still gory from whoever's mouth it had been uprooted from. She was an avid fan of horror movies and many a time I had to check to ensure that "Freddy Cougar" (as she called him) hadn't attached himself to the trunk of my car.

She was a brilliant, wounded soul.

At times, Elisha retreated into Powerland, a complex, sprawl-ing world of her invention, with its own demigod, history, laws, and story. One minute she'd be scaling the monkey bars or spin-ning circles on the tire swing, and the next she'd have slipped away from me, dazed when I pulled her back with the sound of my voice.

"I'll bring you to Powerland soon," she'd promise. "The people there just have to trust you first. They don't know if you're safe. A bad man has come there; everybody is scared."

I knew that Elisha, now eight, was harbouring secrets. One day she told me one of them. "I tried to kill myself yesterday," she confessed. "I stood in front of the bathroom mirror with a knife."

I brought her to my church. She was astonished that people knew me and greeted me by name. She spoke bitterly of God, won-dering how it was that an all-powerful being allowed little girls to suffer.

She was thirteen when her mom kicked her out and she ended up in that first foster home where locks were placed on the refriger-ator door. Over the next few years Elisha would move from foster home to group home to life on the streets, going hungrily from one scene to the next, always searching for something but find-ing only more pain. She would seek refuge in a tent in a ravine. She would be raped more than once, with cruel words scrawled in pen across her body as she lay unconscious. She would be sliced open, a vicious wound up the length of her arm, by a boyfriend in a drug-induced rage. She would grow hard, speak of kicking some girl who had collapsed on the sidewalk, speak of doing meth, of chatting casually with hardened old men who'd spent their lives on the street.

She was so hard and so beautiful all at once, and I grieved that I couldn't do more for this once-upon-a-child.

In her late teens, Elisha got pregnant and gave birth to a son. He softened her, somehow reaching into her and exposing her most tender parts. Hardened though she was, she became his defender, sought out the life for him that she had been denied, celebrated him, and chose well for him. And from the dirt of the streets, from an untold number of dirty mattresses in temporary homes, from a life almost numbed senseless by the number of blows it had received, something beautiful grew.

My little girl, age five, stands tentatively in my doorway, eyes still heavy with sleep. I lift my arm in the old familiar gesture that only she understands.

Michaela leaps into my bed, having no doubt of her rightful place. Nestling down under the quilt next to me, she sighs, "Oh, Mommy!" She chuckles, snuggles up as close as she can get, and turns onto her side to snooze away the last few hours of the early morning. Breathing softly, my girl stretches her legs and pushes her sharp little elbow into my side. Then she relaxes, her body warm and soft and safe against me.

I'm a hurting Mommy, recently on my own. My disintegrating marriage has left me wounded. No matter what I try, I can't make things right. I'm worn down, defeated. But nothing strikes a harder blow than knowing that the children I created with the man I loved will suffer because of us.

I remain awake, comforted by the rhythm of my daughter's chest as it rises and falls. Her softness takes me back to the feeling of baby Samara's body the day I pressed her hard against me before letting her go for good.

It ripped something open in me, losing her. But then one day, when Samara was four and had enough hair to merit barrettes, her adoptive mother brought her for a visit. At first, I just gaped at the child, who was at once familiar and foreign. She had aged (a concept my brain struggled to master), and she had forgotten us, but she was still the same old Samara. She grinned her crooked grin and rubbed her crumpled ears, and then we romped around the basement, my little brother, Samara, and me.

I had seen it then, that glint of hope, the idea that this child had been put into the right arms—our arms, and then the arms of her adoptive mother—when she so badly needed to be loved. I recognized then, at age thirteen, that the beginning of someone's story isn't necessarily the ending. And despite how much losing our foster babies hurt, I knew intuitively that our arms had to be open so that God could place these vulnerable lives right into them.

Strangely enough, I would discover years later that the reverse was also true: God had put my life into the arms of these little ones as they reached out for me. In my twenties I started to remember, fragment by agonizing fragment, the violent abuse I had suffered in the hands of a family friend, unbeknownst to my parents, when I was only a preschooler. As memories surfaced, I came to understand why I had only felt safe at night as a child when I had a baby in my room, another life to share the weight of the darkness pressing in on us.

Those hurting foster babies showed me, early in life, that abuse or neglect in no way reduces a human being's worth. Love is transformative, and God's arms have an uncanny way of grabbing hold of us. I have let him hold me, wounds and all, again and again.

I trace the contour of Michaela's ear as she lies so peacefully next to me. Her vulnerability reminds me of Elisha, age six, waiting by the window in the hope that someone would love her enough to return. I remember the day when she asked me if she could call me "Mommy." I'm so glad I said, "Yes." So glad I'm still in touch with her. So proud of how well she's doing.

Michaela shifts, and groans, and for a moment I'm gripped by how cold this world is, how randomly it dispenses senseless suffering and hope, cruelty and tenderness. I'm shaken by the knowledge that no matter how vigilant I am, I can't protect my sleeping daughter from knowing pain and loss.

And yet, I know the God who sees the baby in her crib staring up at the ceiling; who sees the girl unconscious on a dirty mattress, her skin stained with ink; who sees the five-year-old sound asleep, oblivious to her mother's pain and their uncertain future; who sees this whole hurting and complex mess of humanity and reaches right into it, arms wide open. And I can't tell if the exquisite pain I feel comes from the tragedy or from the beauty that seems to relentlessly emerge.

I slip back into a gentle sleep, firm in the knowledge that from the hardest places, the most beautiful things will grow.

1. Names and some details have been changed to ensure the anonymity of the children in this story.

Boulderdash

 ## Heather McGillivray-Seers

I stand at the bottom of Impossible
and look up;
this is my mountain
moving me,
these are the hard rocks that
mock; make me slide
from their slippery embrace,
monuments towering over me
announcing my demise,
ridiculing,
my Goliath, taunting
turn away.

I have nowhere to go,
this is the way; and so
I scan the parameters;
no sling to bring this giant down,
but here at the base
I pick away at the fallacies,
finding the false pillars,
those smooth sleek lies
propping the whole thing up.

Some mountains come crashing
down with a word,
some go plummeting to the depths
of the sea,
and some can only be moved
one small stone at a time.

  A Taste of Hot Apple Cider

Give thanks
to the LORD,
for He is good;
His love
endures forever.

1 Chronicles 16:34

More Hot Apple Cider books!

Sign up for our New Releases mailing list, and get a FREE epub of *Hot Apple Cider: Words to Warm the Soul and Stir the Heart*, which has more than 40 encouraging stories of faith, hope, and love by 30 Canadian writers.

"A collection of short stories, poetry, and wisdom seeking to heal and mend the soul of the reader after difficult and stressful situations.... Highly recommended."
  —Midwest Book Review

"Much in the tradition of *Chicken Soup for the Soul*... Enjoy!"
  —Brian C. Stiller, Global Ambassador for the World Evangelical Alliance

"Spend an afternoon with *Hot Apple Cider*. It could just change your life."
  —Jane Kirkpatrick, award-winning author

http://hotappleciderbooks.com/subscribe/

Our Contributors

That's Life! Communications thanks the wonderful writers who shared their stories and their hearts. Meet them on the following pages.

A. A. Adourian

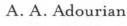

www.aaadourian.com

A. A. Adourian loves to learn about God and write about how the Holy Spirit can change our hearts. She's always asking God for more faith to trust Him, and He gives her plenty of practice! A librarian by profession, with more than a decade of experience in the field, A. A. is a skilled researcher and the author of numerous business-related reports in a corporate environment. She was first published in *A Second Cup of Hot Apple Cider,* and continues to thank God as He challenges her to make Him known by both how she lives and what she writes.

Photo by Darcie Sutherland Photography

Glynis M. Belec

www.glynisbelec.com

Glynis Belec, an award-winning freelance writer, author and private tutor, faces each day with hope and thanksgiving. She rejoices daily and is constantly reminded about looking at the world through child-sized eyes. Glynis loves capturing life in words and can't wait for tomorrow so she can feel inspired all over again.

Jailhouse Rock (Concordia Publishing)
Mrs. B Has Cancer (Angel Hope Publishing)

Vilma Blenman

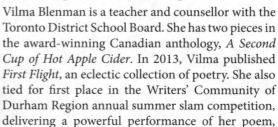

http://writerteacher.wordpress.com

Vilma Blenman is a teacher and counsellor with the Toronto District School Board. She has two pieces in the award-winning Canadian anthology, *A Second Cup of Hot Apple Cider*. In 2013, Vilma published *First Flight*, an eclectic collection of poetry. She also tied for first place in the Writers' Community of Durham Region annual summer slam competition, delivering a powerful performance of her poem, "Fat Girl Feelings." Vilma is a passionate mentor, mother and gardener. She lives with her husband Grantley and their two children in Pickering, Ontario.

  A Taste of Hot Apple Cider

Angelina Fast-Vlaar

www.angelinafastvlaar.com

Award-winning author Angelina Fast-Vlaar was born in Holland and resides in St. Catharines, Ontario. Her writing includes nonfiction books, articles, and poetry. As an inspirational speaker, Angelina draws on her wealth of experience to captivate and motivate audiences. As a cancer survivor, she offers hope and encouragement.

Seven Angels for Seven Days (Castle Quay Books)
The Valley of Cancer: A Journey of Comfort and Hope (Word Alive Press)

Donna Fawcett

http://donnafawcett.com

Donna Fawcett was raised in a Christian home. After realizing, at age 28, that religion and relationship with Christ were not the same thing, she surrendered her life to Jesus. Donna is a former creative writing instructor for Fanshawe College in London, Ontario. Two of her books won The Word Awards for Best Contemporary Novel in 2009 and 2011. Donna speaks for Stonecroft Women's Ministries.

Vengeance (Word Alive Press)
Between Heaven and Earth (New Scroll Books)

Keturah Harris

http://keturahspace.wordpress.com

Keturah Harris has one life mission—inspiring individuals, groups, and organizations to achieve theirs! Whether as an award-winning author, worship leader/speaker, management consultant, educator, or career coach, Keturah's passion for facilitating positive transformation has motivated 100s of students and professionals to identify and wholeheartedly pursue their unique God-given destinies.

Reflections from the Waiting Room: Insights for Thriving When Life Puts You on Hold (Essence)

David Kitz

www.davidkitz.ca

David Kitz is an actor, award-winning author, and ordained minister with the Foursquare Gospel Church of Canada. His love for drama and storytelling is evident to all who have seen his Bible-based performances. He has toured across Canada and the United States with a variety of one-man plays for both children and adults. Born and raised in Saskatchewan, David now lives in Ottawa, Ontario.

Psalms Alive! (Forever Books)
The Soldier, the Terrorist & the Donkey King (Essence Publishing)

N. J. Lindquist

www.njlindquist.com

An award-winning author, inspiring speaker, and empowering teacher, N. J. Lindquist began publishing independently in 2000 after having three royalty publishers. She'll soon have 20 published books, including the coming-of-age Circle of Friends series and the award-winning Manziuk and Ryan mystery series. N. J.'s vision for a community of writers with a Christian faith working together contributed to the founding of The Word Guild. Prairie-bred, N. J. lives in Markham, Ontario.

LoveChild: Reflections From a Former Ugly Duckling (That's Life! Communications) - coming 2015
Shadow of a Butterfly (MurderWillOut Mysteries) - as J. A. Menzies

Heather McGillivray-Seers

http://rapturedheart.wordpress.com

Heather McGillivray-Seers is following Jesus. Sometimes it's an earth's orbit-altering adventure, and sometimes it's harrowing; but always, it's where she wants to be. Sometimes she writes about it. She also has two pieces in the Canadian bestselling anthology, *A Second Cup of Hot Apple Cider.*

Heidi McLaughlin

www.heartconnection.ca

International speaker, author and columnist Heidi McLaughlin believes there is nothing more beautiful than a person who knows they are loved by God. Heidi guides people into this truth through her speaking, mentoring, thought-provoking articles, and intimate conversations over a steaming cup of strong coffee. Heidi lives amidst the beautiful vineyards of West Kelowna, British Columbia.

Beauty Unleashed: Transforming a Woman's Soul (VMI Publishing)
Sand to Pearls: Making Bold Choices to Enrich Your Life (Deep River Books)

Dorene Meyer

www.dorenemeyer.com

Dorene Meyer is the author of eleven novels, two children's books, a reference book, and a life story. She has edited seventeen anthologies: eight with adults, three with teens and six with children. As owner of Goldrock Press, Meyer has also published many books written by authors whom she has mentored. Dorene has won several awards and received various grants for her writing.

Photo by jaygaune.ca

Rachel's Children (Goldrock Press)
Jasmine (Goldrock Press) The Word Awards 2011 Best Romance Novel

Ruth Smith Meyer

www.ruthsmithmeyer.com

Ruth Smith Meyer, a writer and speaker raised in the Stouffville area, now alternates living between Ailsa Craig and Listowel, Ontario. She has published two well-received adult novels and a children's book. As an inspirational speaker, she addresses a wide variety of topics. Ruth also teaches how to positively face death, dying, and the grief journey.

Not Easily Broken and *Not Far from the Tree* (Word Alive Press)
Tyson's Sad Bad Day (Word Alive Press)

Kimberley Payne

www.kimberleypayne.com

Kimberley Payne is a motivational speaker and writer. Her writing relates raising a family, pursuing a healthy lifestyle, and everyday experiences, to building a strong relationship with God. Kimberley, who lives near Peterborough, Ontario, offers practical, guilt-free tips on improving spiritual and physical health. She teaches workshops at churches, women's retreats and conferences.

Photo by Mike Feraco

Fit for Faith (Within Reach)
Where Family Meets Faith (byDesign Media)

Don Ranney, MD

http://personal.uwaterloo.ca/ranney/

Don Ranney, MD, FRCS, went to India in 1969 to help leprosy sufferers through reconstructive surgery. He also trained five surgeons, wrote two medical books, and published 14 scientific papers. Later he established the School of Anatomy at the University of Waterloo, Waterloo, Ontario. Don is currently helping accident-injured people through orthopaedic assessments while continuing his research. He now has 117 published scientific papers.

When Cobras Laugh, with co-author Ray Wiseman (Capstone Fiction)
Life Beyond Life in a Parallel Universe – coming in 2015

Carmen Wittmeier

www.carmenwittmeier.blogspot.com

Carmen Wittmeier completed her MA in English at the University of Alberta in 1999. She has taught English literature at several colleges and worked as an editor, writer, and reporter. Her current passion is advocating for children trafficked into the sex trade. Carmen lives in Calgary, Alberta, with her two daughters and their growing collection of pets.

Affirming the Birth Mother's Journey: A Peer Counselor's Guide to Adoption Counseling (Trafford)

Keep in Touch

If you want to know about new books,
where and when our writers are speaking or signing,
special offers, webinars, and more, please connect with us!

Subscribe to get news and special offers

http://hotappleciderbooks.com/subscribe/

Like us on Facebook

@hotappleciderbooks

Follow us on Twitter

@thatslifecomm

Visit our website

http://hotappleciderbooks.com

Are you part of a book club or small group?

Accompanied by its Discussion Guide, each of the books in the Hot Apple Cider series might be perfect for your book club or small group. Or you might use the questions for personal reflection.

See the Discussion Questions on the next pages.

Discussion Questions

Purpose

For each of the 16 stories and poems, we've provided a set of in-depth discussion questions to help you:

- Think further about the issues raised
- Enjoy stimulating conversations
- Share ideas and meaningful experiences

Who should use these questions?

These questions are the perfect tool either for private study or for study within a group.

- **Individual Readers:** Use the questions to meditate on the issues raised by each article, then write down your responses.
- **Book Clubs:** The pieces in this anthology are diverse, and everyone in your book club is bound to find something enjoyable. Also, the pieces are short, so you can easily talk about a number of them in one evening. Book club leaders can use some or all of the questions in this guide to drive the discussion about each piece.
- **Small Groups:** Whichever kind of small group you are in—a discussion group, adult class, men's or women's group, or a support group for people facing issues such as illness or bereavement—you'll find material that will interest and benefit its members. Many stories and questions include scripture references.
- **Speakers, Pastors, Teachers:** The stories in this book provide wonderful material for a talk, sermon, devotional, or group discussion. The questions in this guide are designed to give you insights and offer additional scripture references that you can use in your talk.

Subway Surprise

by A. A. Adourian

God is ever-present, despite distractions and our feelings of being alone.

1. The writer's search for answers was met with a simple message: "God loves you."

   a) How did that message change her attitude toward her problems?

   b) What was your reaction to the way God spoke to her?

2. The writer experiences God's love in an extraordinary way, but through an ordinary person. Can you recall having a similar experience where you felt God spoke to you through a stranger?

3. Describe one occasion when you put your faith in God even when He seemed distant, and then were surprised, even delighted, by the outcome.

  A Taste of Hot Apple Cider

4. Recall a time when God asked you to share something (a Bible verse, a prayer, a helping hand, a room, a meal, some money...).

   a) If you shared something, what was the other person's reaction?

   b) If you didn't share, what stopped you?

5. Even if you've never been on a subway, you've likely seen them in movies or on TV. In rush hours in particular, there are a lot of people in each other's space, day after day, each person with his or her own story.

   a) Write down some other settings when strangers, all with unique stories, are in close quarters for brief or long periods of time.

   b) Brainstorm ways you might intentionally share in some of these people's stories.

6. Early in the story, the writer reflects on the meaning of "community."

   a) How is our idea of community changing in our digital age?

   b) How has that affected you?

Love Has No Limits

by Donna Fawcett

A daughter reacts to her elderly widowed father's need for romance.

1. It's been said elderly people only look old; they don't necessarily feel any different than when they were younger. The writer certainly noticed that with her father.

   a) What was your feeling when you realized this story was essentially a romance?

   b) How does the realization that eighty-year-olds can act like teenagers change the way you think of older people?

2. Before her death, the writer's mother gave permission to her husband to get involved with someone else. Do you think you'd be willing to give the same permission to a spouse? Why or why not?

3. If you were in a similar position to the writer's, how might you respond to a widowed parent's romance?

4. If you were that lonely older person, how do you think your own family would react to your seeking romance?

5. Have you ever tried matchmaking? If so, how did it turn out? If not, why not?

6. Bell lost her new husband within a year. How do you think she felt about getting involved with Ed?

7. Loneliness is a real problem for the elderly. While not everyone might be looking for a new romance, we all long to have at least one other person who is genuinely interested in us. How might a family member or friend ease the loneliness of an older person?

8. People who have never married may also face increased loneliness as they grow older and become less mobile. And, the truth is, the older you are, the more of your friends need extra care or pass away. What might individuals or churches do to help?

9. Are there community centres, organizations for elderly people, or other social groups in your area that you could recommend?

Something to Crow About

by David Kitz

A remarkable encounter with a crow speaks deeply to our human needs.

1. The writer gives us a detailed insight into his opinion of crows.

   a) Before reading this story, what was your opinion of crows?

   b) Has your opinion changed after reading this account?

2. The story describes a special interaction with an animal.

   a) Can you recall a memorable experience where you felt a bird or other wild animal communicated with you in some way?

   b) What about a pet?

3. The crow was very annoying, but a moment of vulnerability changed the writer's perception of the bird. Share an experience where a moment of vulnerability between you and another person who annoyed you changed your relationship.

4. How does it make you feel when the superiority of our species is challenged by the actions of an animal?

5. In the writer's opinion, the crow returned to thank a human for his kindness.

   a) How do you tend to express gratitude for the kindness you are shown by others?

   b) Why is it often difficult for us to thank others for their kindnesses toward us?

6. The writer found the crow's cawing much less annoying after this incident. In fact, he welcomed it.

   a) What might this suggest about how our attitude might change toward people who annoy us?

   b) Without naming names, think of a person you found abrasive at first, but learned to appreciate. What changed your mind?

Desperate Missionary in Trouble with the Law

by Don Ranney, MD

A missionary makes a dramatic trip to get back home in time for a funeral.

1. While a missionary doctor, the writer "broke" or "bent" several laws in order to get home in time for his father's funeral.

   a) How do you feel about what he did?

   b) Was the missionary a good or a bad example to the people he was working with? Why?

2. Many of us come to a place where we have to weigh our obedience to our own instincts, God's laws, and human laws.

   a) Did the writer cause any harm by breaking the law?

   b) How do we decide when the end justifies the means?

3. What other options might the writer have had?

4. A lot of things worked out for him in an extraordinary way for the writer to make his trip. Share a time when things worked out for you in an unexpected way.

5. Ultimately, the writer was able to get to Canada because the Hindu people he worked with honoured their parents and elders. How might things have been different where you live?

6. The missionary was considered to be in India to "corrupt the minds of good Hindus and turn them into Christians."

   a) Was he really corrupting their minds, or acting out of love and respect for them?

   b) Do missionaries need to show great love and respect in order to have influence?

   c) What implication might that have for us when we think about sharing our faith with our neighbours and others in our community?

A Time to Have Tea

by Vilma Blenman

A working mother tries to keep up her normal life while fighting cancer.

1. The writer is determined to carry on with her full-time teaching and counselling job while undergoing daily radiation treatment for cancer. Why do you think this would be important to her?

2. She is exasperated by her exhaustion rather than taking cues from it and slowing down. Can you recall a time when you kept going in spite of your exhaustion?

3. Ironically, the writer seems reluctant to let other people help her.

   a) Why do so many people refuse to admit they need help?

   b) Share a time when you let somebody help you. How did it turn out?

4. Recognizing the need to enjoy a cup of tea was important. What might you do in order to take a break and be refreshed?

5. Do you consciously practice self-care? If so, can you share a few of your principles?

6. What is the role of friends and family members in helping each other practice self-care?

7. How can parents teach their children the art of practical compassionate care for others?

8. Cancer touches so many of our own lives in one way or another.

    a) What are some "dabs of honey" that someone struggling with cancer or another illness may need?

    b) What are some possible needs of their family members?

9. In the story, women from the writer's small group at church help provide rides for her to radiation therapy. How does your church community know of and respond to similar needs?

In His Shoes

by Keturah Harris

A final walk with her ailing father leads a woman to a place of grace.

1. Impending death has a way of putting things in perspective.

   a) In what ways can you relate to the writer's change in her perception of her father?

   b) In what ways might a new perspective help (or have helped) in your relationship with your mother or father?

2. Our relationships with our parents change as we mature.

   a) Share an example of how your connection with one or both of your parents changed.

   b) What words would you use to describe the way you deal with (or dealt) with your parent(s)?

3. How close is (or was) your relationship with your parent(s) to your ideals and values?

4. How might humour or forgiveness help you re-frame the way you assess your parent(s)?

5. How is it possible to accept a parent or other family member who falls and needs to be "caught" without condoning the fallen behaviour?

6. What might you need to change, accept, or let go of in order to experience peace and extend grace to your parent(s)?

7. We all fall at some point in our lives.

a) If you feel comfortable, share an example of a time when someone "caught" you when you fell.

b) How did you respond at the time?

c) What does it mean to you now?

The Ring

by Angelina Fast-Vlaar

The wife of an Alzheimer patient faces a new milestone in his illness.

1. What emotions does this poem evoke in you?

2. The writer documents another stage downward in the progression of the dementia which has taken hold of her husband.

    a) How is the dementia affecting the patient?

    b) How is her husband's dementia affecting the caregiver?

    c) Is there someone in your life going through a similar illness?

    d) Why is it somehow easier to talk about an illness that attacks the body than one that attacks the brain?

3. Where is this particular caregiver finding the strength to carry on?

4. What do we learn about life from this piece?

5. The narrator is given the gift of a moment of lucidity from her husband as he jokes with her. What do you suppose that meant to her?

The Right Thing to Do

by Ruth Smith Meyer

A couple responds to a young woman's distress on a lonely country road.

1. In the opening of this story, the writer expresses a desire to make a difference.

   a) Have you shared that feeling?

   b) What have you done about it?

2. What do you think your first reaction would have been had you come across the scene the people in the story encountered?

3. There was certainly a risk in the action that was taken.

   a) How do you think her earlier prayer influenced their response to the situation?

   b) What would you have done differently from the writer and her husband?

4. The writer says, "Be careful what you pray for." Share a time when you prayed for something and found the answer overwhelming.

5. How easy or difficult is it for you to trust God to guide you in emergencies?

6. Can you recall a situation where you had to make a quick decision? Did you do the right thing or do you wish you had done something different?

7. The sexual assault was handled outside the police system.

    a) What factors might have come into that decision?

    b) Do you think they should have tried to convince the young woman to tell the police? Why or why not?

    c) If you feel they should have gone to the police, how might they have handled that, especially since the victim was unwilling?

Everybody Needs a Friend Who'll Tell It Like It Is

by Heidi McLaughlin

A woman realizes that we are created for authentic, intimate relationships.

1. The initial story is centred on what to do when a friend hurts us.

   a) Why do you think Heidi wouldn't have confronted her friend Aimee if her other friend Maureen hadn't reminded her?

   b) When a friend hurts us, we essentially have two choices. We can walk away and let go of the friendship, or we can talk about it, and try to keep the friend. Which of these two paths are you most likely to take?

   c) What are a few ways to confront a person lovingly?

   d) What does it mean to you to know there are people you can be yourself with, who will pray for you and have your back even when you make mistakes?

2. The writer describes her close friendship with two other women.

   a) If you've ever had a friendship like that of the members of the Sacred Sock Sisterhood, share a little about how it worked.

b) How easy is it for you to be truthful and authentic ("spiritually naked and not ashamed") with other people?

c) If it's hard, what is it you fear?

3. In this story, the writer refers to the "one another" principles.

    I. "Let us not become conceited, provoking and envying each other" (Galatians 5:26).

    II. "Let us consider how we may spur one another on toward love and good deeds" (Hebrews 10:24).

    III. "Therefore encourage one another with these words" (1 Thessalonians 4:18).

    IV. "Accept one another, then, just as Christ accepted you, in order to bring praise to God" (Romans 15:7).

    V. "Therefore confess your sins to each other and pray for each other so that you may be healed" (James 5:16a).

a) Which of these "one another's" do you find the easiest to follow?

b) Which of them do you need the most work on?

c) How might you work on improving?

4. If you don't have accountability partners, but would like to, how might you create a small group like the Sacred Sock Sisterhood?

Picture This!

by Kimberley Payne

A woman finds a way to spread God's message of love in her neighbourhood.

1. The writer wanted to reach out to get to know her neighbours, but was afraid of how they would react to her.

   a) What did you think of the way she eventually found to do it?

   b) Why are some people afraid to reach out to strangers while others interact easily with almost everyone they meet?

   c) What kind of fear has stopped you from reaching out to get to know others?

   d) How did you manage to overcome the fear? Or did it win?

2. Share about a time when you met a neighbour under unusual circumstances and felt it was God's doing.

  A Taste of Hot Apple Cider

3. When the writer did overcome her fear, it was ironic that the neighbour was like-minded.

   a) Do you think this was an accident or might God have a sense of humour?

   b) Share a time when you saw God's humour in a situation.

4. Tell about a time when you deliberately stepped out of your comfort zone and were blessed by it.

5. The writer used a hobby she enjoyed as a way of connecting with her neighbours. What interests do you have that you might share with one or more neighbours?

My Love Affair with Gym

by Glynis Belec

A late-night accident in an empty gym becomes a God-moment.

1. Some things seem insignificant when we're dealing with more serious issues. Who really cares about weight gain when we're facing cancer? Yet, as holistic people, we need to balance everything.

   a) What excuse did the writer use to justify her weight gain?

   b) How valid would you say her excuse was?

2. By indulging in things we know are bad for us or not doing things we know we ought to do, we can endanger our health.

   a) Share a time when you failed to take responsibility for something that you could control.

   b) When you eventually did take responsibility, how did you feel?

   c) Did the situation become better once you faced up to it?

   d) Is there something in your life right now that you need to take control of?

3. The writer managed to find humour in the midst of a painful experience. Share how laughing helped you deal with a difficult situation. (Or did you only find it funny looking back at it?)

4. Sometimes God gets our attention in unusual ways. Have you ever experienced a time when God sent you a message in an unexpected circumstance?

5. What scars do you have (physical or psychological) that remind you about how God was there for you in a situation, encouraging you to persevere?

6. Have you ever dreaded doing something, but once you took the plunge, discovered you loved it? Share a little about how this changed your outlook of life in general.

7. Most of us know someone who is struggling.

   a) Do you know anyone who could use encouragement to keep from giving up?

   b) What might you be able to do to help?

My Journey to Joy

by Dorene Meyer

A strong Christian finds her joy tempered by sadness.

1. The writer believes she should feel joyful because she knows God loves her, but most of the time she struggles with deep sadness. She mentions three areas C. S. Lewis referred to in his book, *Surprised by Joy*, and adds another of her own.

   a) Can you add to this list of things that can take away from our joy—even just the joy of being alive?

   • Early childhood trauma

   • Pessimistic attitudes and words from a parent

   • Frustration with one's physical abilities

   • Knowledge of how many people in the world are struggling

   •

   •

   •

   •

   b) Our past experiences colour the way we see life. What have you done to deal with, rather than deny, negative experiences?

2. Joy is a difficult word to define.

   a) What's the difference between having joy because God loves you and being an optimist who always sees the glass as half full?

b) Why should (or shouldn't) a Christian always be an optimist?

3. Obesity and related health issues are becoming epidemic in North America. Why do you think so many people, like the writer, struggle with weight-related issues?

4. As the writer indicated, it's possible to know joy in the midst of sadness. Share one occasion when you experienced both joy and sadness at the same time.

5. Not everyone shows joy the same way. How do you express joy?

6. We can't ignore that many people today live in overwhelming, heart-breaking situations.

a) What are a few ways we can adequately respond to some of the many needs around the world?

b) What is one thing you could do to address a specific need in your community?

Loving Play

by Vilma Blenman

Scenes of a child at play highlight the contrasts in parents' attitudes.

1. Play is a God-given instinct, something present in all cultures and in both human and animal worlds. But not everyone values it. After reading this poem, describe your feelings toward the following:

   a) The mother of the little boy

   b) The writer of the poem

   c) The writer's mother

2. Think back to your own childhood.

   a) What were your parents' attitudes toward play?

   b) What kinds of play were encouraged and what kinds were off-limits?

   c) How did gender play a role in your parents' play principles?

3. Why do you suppose God gave us the gift of play?

A Taste of Hot Apple Cider

4. Share an experience from your childhood when you did something that got you dirty, or might have seemed dangerous. Did your parents find out? If so, how did they react?

5. It's easy to feel jealous when watching someone else—even one's own child—have fun. How can we learn to appreciate it, like the mother in this poem did?

6. Parents today seem much more protective than in earlier years. Is the world more dangerous or are parents just more cautious?

7. Many parents fill up every minute of their children's time with classes, sports, and other organized activities. How can parents justify giving their child time to do "nothing?"

8. What kind of things do you do for play now that you're an adult?

9. As a parent, aunt, uncle, grandparent, or family friend, how do you engage in play with the child or children in your life?

Conversations in Baby Blue

by N. J. Lindquist

A teen mother grows up quickly when she becomes responsible for another life.

1. Hailey decided to put Austin up for adoption.

   a) Choosing to allow one's child to be adopted is never easy. Do you feel Hailey made a selfish decision or a selfless one? Why?

   b) Given what you've seen of Hailey, her family, and Tyler, do you think this was the best decision for Austin?

   c) How do you feel Hailey's relationships with her family, Tyler, and her friends would change after this?

2. If Hailey had kept Austin:

   a) What problems might have arisen?

   b) What might the good outcomes have been?

3. There were clear indications that Ty wasn't mature enough to be a father/husband. How do you think he would have ultimately responded to Hailey's decision to give the baby up for adoption?

4. In the end, Hailey trusted God to look after Austin.

   a) How difficult would it be to trust God to look after the baby, when a mother's instinct is to protect?

   b) Have you ever admitted you couldn't look after a person, and given him or her into God's care?

5. Nowadays, thousands of babies are aborted each year. How might better promotion of adoption help decrease these numbers?

6. Many people who adopt prefer babies or very young children. However, there are many older children who need homes. What might churches do to encourage members to look at adoption as a way of making a difference?

7. What agencies do you know of that assist unwed mothers?

From Hard Places

by Carmen Wittmeier

*Three portraits of suffering reveal God's redemptive hand
in even the bleakest circumstances.*

1. The name "Samara" comes from the name for a tree seed pod.

   a) How does this meaning enhance the story?

   b) What do the names "Elisha" and "Michaela" suggest to you?

2. Why do you suppose Elisha chose the name "Powerland" for the imaginary world she created?

3. What role do doors play in these portrayals of suffering?

4. The writer describes a time when she was young and "reckless enough to believe that one person could change a life, dismantle the system, transform the world." In your opinion, does this statement simply reflect the idealism of youth, or do we all need to be more reckless?

5. Sooner or later, we all have hard places in our lives.

   a) If you feel comfortable, describe a few of the hard places in your own life.

   b) What beautiful things have grown from your suffering?

6. Intentional love helped turn these potentially tragic circumstances into stories of beauty. What are some ways people can demonstrate intentional love?

7. Many foster parents care very much and invest themselves in the children's lives, only to have to give up the children after a time. How do you feel about the idea of becoming a foster parent?

8. Any time we step out of our comfort zone to care for someone else, we risk loss or even rejection. How is the possibility of pain balanced by the joy of knowing you made, or tried to make, a positive difference in another person's life?

Boulderdash

by Heather McGillivray-Seers

Some mountains must be dismantled one stone at a time.

1. The writer compares the mountain in front of her to the giant Goliath, an experienced warrior who taunted the young shepherd boy, David.

   a) Recall a time when you felt like David, facing a Goliath that seemed too much for you.

   b) Share about at least one mountain that you've moved over the years.

   c) Can you recall a time when a mountain moved you?

2. Some mountains are just a pile of lies we've believed over the years, many of which came into our lives when we were young. Can you add to this list of lies?

   - There's nothing you can do...
   - It's too hard for you...
   - No one else cares; why should you...
   - No one likes/loves you...
   - You're not as (pretty, smart, well-behaved, strong...) as...
   -
   -
   -
   -

3. Which three lies have had the most influence on you over the years?

-

-

-

4. Has there been a time in your life when God completely dismantled your mindset about something? How did you feel afterwards?

5. Moving mountains one stone at a time still requires faith. There are some aspects of every problem that we need to leave in God's hands. How are you working with God to move a mountain you are facing right now?

6. Could some mountains move us in a positive direction? Give an example.

7. What impossible mountain(s) are you facing at this moment?

Acknowledgements

I'm delighted to have another opportunity to showcase work by some Canadian writers who are Christian. They were a pleasure to work with.

Thank you to everyone who sent in submissions. There were so many good stories! I wish I could have used them all.

Thank you to the writers whose work is in *A Taste of Hot Apple Cider*. Thank you for choosing to put your stories into words in the first place and for not going ballistic when I tore into your precious words. I especially appreciate those of you who thanked me for doing it! It was a pleasure to work with all of you.

Thanks to my husband and business partner, Les Lindquist, for going through the submissions with me and helping me make the selections, for doing some substantive editing, and for all his work in creating some of the discussion questions and editing the rest. Who knew that was something he'd enjoy?

A ton of thanks to Grace Fox who, in spite of being super busy, generously agreed to write the foreword to this book. Thanks so much, Grace!

Thanks to Ingrid Paulson, of Ingrid Paulson Design, who designed the first two covers.

Thanks to all the contributors who checked the final drafts and sent in things they caught.

Thanks especially to Heather McGillivray-Seers, Marguerite Cummings, Claire Alexander, and A. A. Adourian for their help with copyediting and proofreading.

Most important, thank God for making it possible for me to work with Canadian writers who are eager to learn and grow in their expertise. Please be sure to read their bios on pages 104-108.

My prayer is that each reader will be both encouraged and inspired through the words on these pages—and maybe just a little bit challenged.

N. J. Lindquist

Hot Apple Cider

If you enjoyed *A Taste of Hot Apple Cider*, **you'll want to read the rest of the books in the series.**

44 stories of faith and inspiration

Trade paperback and digital

"A collection of short stories, poetry, and wisdom seeking to heal and mend the soul of the reader after difficult and stressful situations.... Highly recommended..."
Midwest Book Review

"This is a book to sample, to savour, and to share."
Maxine Hancock, PhD, Professor Emeritus, Regent College; author

Winner, five The Word Awards

Winner, Church Library Association of Ontario One Book/One Conference

Available from most bookstores and online.

A Second Cup of Hot Apple Cider

51 stories of hope and encouragement
Trade paperback and digital

"Some books surprise you with their ability to take your breath away.... Be sure to buy more than one, for you will probably have the urge to share this gem of a collection with others."
Faith Today

Winner, thirteen The Word Awards

Winner, Christian Small Publisher Gift Book of the Year Award

Winner, third place, The Book Club Network, Inc. Book of the Year Award

Available from most bookstores and online.

Hot Apple Cider with Cinnamon

67 stories of unexpected love and caring
Trade paperback and digital

Available from most bookstores and online.

Visit our website for more information:
- Reviews and endorsements
- Website links and interviews with contributing writers
- News about upcoming books and author signings

http://hotappleciderbooks.com

Need a Gift?

Many people have told us they've bought additional copies of this book or the other Hot Apple Cider books to give to family members or friends. We've also heard from a number of people who were delighted to be given a book.

If you've enjoyed this book, please consider giving a copy of it or one of the other Hot Apple Cider books to someone else who might need encouragement.

You can even order bulk copies from the publisher at a special discount for use as gifts to employees, friends and family, or those in need; or as a fundraiser in your church/community.

http://thatslifecommunications.com/bulk-copies/

Individual print copies of all the Hot Apple Cider books are available from your local bookstore or online.

Publisher

That's Life! Communications

Books that integrate real faith with real life

That's Life! Communications is a niche publisher committed to finding innovative ways to produce quality books written by Canadians with a Christian faith perspective.

http://thatslifecommunications.com

We'd love to hear your comments about this book or any of our other books. Please post a comment on our website or write to us at:

comments@thatslifecommunications.com